MUSTIKA KWITANG

PAMUR

BHAKTI NEGARA

MADURA

BALI

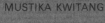

TJIMANDE

PENTJAK - SILAT

The Indonesian Fighting Art

PENTJAK - SILAT
The Indonesian Fighting Art

by
Howard Alexander
Quintin Chambers
Donn F. Draeger

講談社

Published by
KODANSHA INTERNATIONAL LTD.
Tokyo, New York & San Francisco

Distributors:

UNITED STATES: Harper & Row, Publishers, Inc.
10 East 53rd Street, New York, New York 10022

CANADA: Fitzhenry & Whiteside Limited
150 Lesmill Road, Don Mills, Ontario

CENTRAL AND SOUTH AMERICA: Feffer & Simons Inc.
31 Union Square, New York, New York 10003

BRITISH COMMONWEALTH (excluding Canada and the Far
East): TABS
51 Weymouth Street, London W1

EUROPE: Boxerbooks Inc.
Limmatstrasse 111, 8031 Zurich, Switzerland

THAILAND: Central Department Store Ltd.
306 Silom Road, Bangkok

HONG KONG: Books for Asia Ltd.
379 Prince Edward Road, Kowloon

THE FAR EAST: Japan Publications Trading Company
P.O. Box 5030, Tokyo International, Tokyo

JAPAN: Kodansha International Ltd.
2–12–21 Otowa, Bunkyo-ku, Tokyo 112

Published by Kodansha International Ltd., 2–12–21 Otowa, Bunkyo-ku, Tokyo 112 and Kodansha International/USA Ltd., 10 East 53rd Street, New York, New York 10022 and 44 Montgomery Street, San Francisco, California 94104.

LCC 73-82659
ISBN 0-87011-104-3
JBC 2075-781039-2361

First edition, 1970
Third printing, 1973

Contents

Preface

What we present in this book is an introductory approach to the fascinating but relatively little-known combative art of Indonesia that is called "pentjak-silat." We shall outline briefly the background and essentials of the art and then the technical characteristics of some major pentjak-silat styles. In presenting a composite, overall picture of various tactics and training methods, we will illustrate the features that are intrinsic to the art, but we shall not attempt an exhaustive treatment of any one style.

To the beginner, pentjak-silat may appear to be identical with—or at any rate highly similar to—what has come to be popularly known as "karate" (more correctly, *karate-dō* or *karate-jutsu*). There are, however, many technical differences between the two arts, though both, it is true, feature the many ways a man may use his body to dodge or ward off attacks as well as the many ways he may retaliate against an attack by striking or kicking his assailant. To the untrained eye, these will appear to be similar actions, and although they in fact are not, pentjak-silat remains of special interest to karate enthusiasts.

By studying the book carefully and then by practicing the

exercises, the reader will soon become aware of some of these technical differences. Although this knowledge is in itself of value, the distinctions will constitute only separate, acquired skills unless they are integrated through a formal study of pentjak-silat. Further, when these techniques are added to a substantial basic knowledge of karate, they form a source for surprisingly new and useful abilities both in original combat situations and in sport.

We began, necessarily, where all orthodox pentjak-silat training does—with empty-hand skills, and continued on to armed combat. In our study, we were faced with various difficulties. For one thing, the Indonesian climate can be a trying one; and for another, transportation in remote areas is uncertain. Sometimes, because of that fact, we were able to view much excellent technique only once, when we would have liked to study it far more thoroughly. Nonetheless, one of our major problems in compiling the book was that of selection. Although we investigated some sixty major pent-jak-silat styles, space limitations have permitted us to deal explicitly with only about ten. We chose, naturally, those that seemed to us to be the most interesting and useful —and we hope that the reader will agree.

All the technical data that follows, as well as the photographs, were obtained by the authors in Java, Madura, Sumatra, and Bali, from native experts and exponents of the art, to all of whom we would like to express our grateful acknowledgement, as well as to the many government officials who assisted us: without the unlimited hospitality they extended to us, and without the generous use of their facilities, this book would not have been possible. Specifically, we would like to express our thanks to Mr. Dirtmoatdjo and the members of Perisai Diri, to George Pantouw, to Dr. Go Yauw Liem and family, to Colonel Sunarjo, Bambang Soedarjanto Jr., to Heiro T.H.S., to Mr. and Mrs. The, to Mr. Atma of Tjimande, to all officials and members of Mustika Kwitang and Tjingkrik, on Java; to Mr. Swetja

8

and the members of Perisai Diri, to Mr. Ida Bagus Oka Diwangkara and Mr. Alit and other officials of Bhakti Negara, on Bali; to Hasan Hubudin of Pamur and his group on Madura; to Mr. Amir Gunawan, Mr. Yusaf Munir, to Mr. Alikusuma, to Mr. Cheam Gek Chin, to Mr. Gan Ho Lay, to Mr. Munap Malin Mudo and the members of Patai, to Mr. Sjech Barinjin, Mr. Rasul Hamdi, Mr. Harum Said, Mr. Djarios, and Mr. Mendang of IPSI, and all the officers and members of Kumango, Baru, and Harimau organizations in Sumatra.

Howard Alexander
Quintin Chambers
Donn F. Draeger

Djakarta
September 1968

Pentjak-silat
Past and Present

Doubtless the earliest men, as prehistoric immigrants to the islands now known as Indonesia, had methods of self-defense. Perhaps at first these primitive peoples were primarily concerned with self-defense against wild animals. Later, as their wanderings took them into different areas, they came into unavoidable contact with other peoples—some unfriendly—and defense against humans became necessary.

Art objects and artifacts show that, by about the eighth century A.D., specific systems of combative measures had been evolved and were operative in the Riouw Archipelago, which lies between Sumatra and the Malay Peninsula. Such systems, however crude, were greatly influenced by various continental Asian cultures, and spread as fighting arts into Indonesia. The Menangkabau people of Sumatra took these early fighting arts and developed them into a particular Indonesian style. One of the earliest powerful kingdoms, that of Srivijaja in Sumatra, from the seventh to the fourteenth centuries, was able to extend its rule by means of the efficiency of its fighting skills.

The civilizations of eleventh century Java developed a wider range of weapons and fighting arts that reached technical perfection under the Majapahit kings of the thirteenth to sixteenth centuries. Originally these fighting arts were the exclusive property of Indonesia's noble ruling class, which kept them a closely guarded secret. But gradually members of the peasantry acquired the skills and were responsible for developing them to a high degree of efficiency. These orthodox systems came in time to be known collectively as pentjak-silat.

The consensus of expert opinion is that the expression "pentjak-silat" literally infers "to fight artfully." But this is not complete enough, nor is it descriptive enough to convey the full meaning of this art. It is essential to understand that pentjak-silat is based on the meaning of its two components. One, *pentjak*, is a training method for self-defense: it consists of a wide range of controlled body movements directed to that purpose. *Silat*, the second component, is the application of the training method—the actual fight. There can be no silat without pentjak. On the other hand, pentjak without silat skills as its objective is purposeless.

Indonesian pentjak-silat is little known in the West. Those who see it for the first time may perhaps make a rough comparison with the better known Japanese (or Okinawan) *karate-dō*, Korean *taekwon-dō*, or even the Chinese *ch'uan-fa* methods. But such comparisons are inaccurate with regard to the techniques. Through a careful study of this book some of the technical differences which mark pentjak-silat apart from other fighting forms will become apparent. For the moment, it is enough to realize that pentjak-silat was developed exclusively by Indonesians, who regard it as an intrinsic part of their cultural heritage. It therefore deserves to be described in its own terms and judged by its own standards.

The primary purpose of pentjak-silat is always self-defense. No conscious effort is made to make orthodox pentjak-silat a system of physical education or a sport. Pentjak-silat's technical fundamentals deal with the use of weapons; no combatant is ever required to enter combat relying only on his empty hands. Therefore weapons of all kinds are studied and applied to combat situations. These weapons may be anatomical, as in *karate-dō* (fist, elbow, knee, foot), or they may be implements (sword, stick, staff, club, knife, and others). Pentjak-silat has an additional peculiarity in that virtually all movements performed empty handed may be performed equally fluently and safely when the combatant is armed. This is not true of present-day Japanese *karate-dō*, though it may be found in many earlier orthodox forms of combat on the Asian continent and in Okinawa.

All pentjak-silat is traditionally evasive. Its characteristic responses to an attack are light, fast, deceptive movements; it seeks to avoid bone-crushing contact with the assailant's charge. Customarily it does not oppose the force of the assailant but rather blends with it and directs it along specific channels where it may then be controlled, allowing the assailant to be eventually subdued. Thus, by long tradition, it is usually defensive in application: the pentjak-silat exponent prefers to await the attacker's moves before taking action. However, this is not an absolute condition by any means.

Almost all pentjak-silat technique operates as a "soft" or "elastic" style of fighting—alert, responsive and adaptive, ready to neutralize whatever aggression it encounters. It has an easily recognized, peculiar, pulsating tempo. In fact, although it is not essential to the proper performance of pentjak movements, percussion music frequently accompanies training exercises. This is done primarily for much the same reason that the musician makes use of a metronome, but with pentjak-silat the music has the further effect of heightening the emotional atmosphere of the training, rather as war drums affect tribal warriors.

Almost all pentjak-silat movements are based on characteristic movements of animals or people. Thus, it is not uncommon to find that the action of a particular style bears some such title as *pendeta* ("priest"), or *garuda* ("eagle"), or *madju kakikiri harimau* ("taking a tigerlike stance"). A couple of other delightfully descriptive titles are *lompat sikap naga* ("jumping in dragon style") and *lompat putri bersidia* ("jumping like a princess and standing near"). The suggested femininity in the latter title is misleading; counterattacks delivered by this method can be astonishingly fierce.

As has already been suggested, pentjak-silat, being a true fighting art, makes no use of warming-up or preparatory exercises, for it recognizes that under fighting conditions a man will have neither time nor opportunity to warm up. As actions preliminary to more energetic drills, pentjak-silat uses directly related and instantly convertible movements that are of silat value. Isolated actions or exercises of the calisthenic type are considered meaningless and unnecessary.

In fact, an exponent of pentjak-silat is trained to be ready to ward off an attack at any time; his body must be flexible enough to make an instantaneous response. Crouching stances and smooth movements into and out of low postures require the exponent to be both extremely strong and flexible in his legs and hips—qualities that can be developed to their fullest only when pentjak-silat is accepted as a way of life. Indonesians make daily use of the full squat posture, a posture that, as anyone knows who has tried it, requires well-developed and flexible leg muscles. Some of the stances and postures of pentjak-silat make greater physical demands than those of Japanese *karate-dō*: they will thus be found to offer an interesting and useful challenge to advocates of *karate-dō*.

The notion that pentjak-silat was evolved solely for use by slight, small-boned people is a mistaken one. While it is indeed ideally suited to the needs of short, slender fighters, many of its most remarkable exponents, like the mountain dwellers of Sumatra, Java, and Bali, are large bodied.

Some one hundred and fifty different pentjak-silat styles

14

can be identified in the three thousand islands that comprise Indonesia and stretch across as many miles from the Indian Ocean in the west to Australian New Guinea in the east. The world's largest archipelago, Indonesia, extends between the Southeast Asian mainland and the Philippines to the north and Australia in the south, and, throughout this vast expanse, pentjak-silat is to be found in both its pure orthodox form and in various combinations and with various modifications.

All these modified forms have technical similarities, but over the centuries they have developed differently and now have their own traditions and identities—in large part the result of a combination of social and geographical influences. Just why this should be true will not be easy to understand until the subject is studied from that precise point of view, but, for the purpose of these preliminary notes, it will be sufficient to list four distinct characteristics of pentjak-silat that are dominant in the following geographical regions:

Sumatra	foot and leg tactics (Harimau, Patai, Baru, Kumango styles)
West Java	hand and arm tactics (Tjimande, Tjingrik, Mustika Kwitang styles)
Central Java	synthesis of arm and leg tactics (Setia Hati style)
East Java, Bali, Madura	synthesis of arm and leg tactics plus grappling methods (Perisai Diri, Bhakti Negara, Pamur styles)

Although pentjak-silat is practiced today by all classes of

15

Indonesian society, the people of the *kampong* ("village") take to it most readily. It may be seen in the remotest jungle or mountain village and on the most inaccessible island; hardly a schoolboy (or girl, for that matter) is without some ability to demonstrate the particular style practiced in the region they live in.

There are no national standards by which the great diversity of styles may be regulated, nor any nationwide organization to further the development of pentjak-silat, although efforts are being made on a minor scale—largely by exponents of unorthodox systems—to produce and popularize it as a national "sport." It seems unlikely that these efforts will succeed: the changeover from genuine self-defense to a sport entails too severe a loss of combative reality and a negation of the actual purpose and function of this art.

Since pentjak-silat was intended for instantaneous use in the emergencies of daily life, the costume used is simply that normally worn, and this remains true today of many of the styles. Others, however, perhaps through reasons of economy as much as anything else, have developed a special training suit. There is no overall standard; each style that has designed a special suit has incorporated in it certain unique features. The reader may decide, following the photographs in this book, to make his own training suit, but the matter is of little practical importance; any costume, such as that used for judo or *karate-dō* exercises, will be found satisfactory.

The spirit of combat, of actual fighting—in other words, silat—must underlie all orthodox pentjak-silat training. Any other attitude negates the meaning of the art. For that reason, trainees practicing together are called "enemies," not mere opponents, and each should regard the other as someone who is trying to take his life. If you train alone, you train against an imaginary enemy or enemies; if you train with a partner, you must always think of him as an enemy.

The emphasis in pentjak-silat is spiritual rather than

16

physical; more so than the emphasis in the fighting arts of Japan (*bugei* as opposed to *budō* forms). That is to say, the soul or the heart of the fighter is of the utmost importance. His purity, or his lack of it, will be reflected in his techniques; experts claim they can read the nature of the trainee's heart simply by watching him practice. For that reason, pentjak-silat is not the activist discipline that the fighting arts of Japan are: it places tremendous importance on the attainment of self-perfection by means other than its own physical techniques.

Yet in spite of its spirituality, pentjak-silat is, quite obviously, founded on the harsh reality of possibly deadly hand-to-hand combat, and in its exercises it imposes the rigors of a real combat situation upon trainees. They are expected to consider not only the weapons being used but also the climate, the time of day or night, and the terrain upon which the combat occurs; these all combine to establish the prevailing emotional as well as physical atmosphere of the fight. Trainees must always bear in mind that the weapons they are using are real objects capable of inflicting serious injury.

NOTE: The authors have avoided, so far as possible, the use of Indonesian to identify and describe the intricacies of the various pentjak-silat techniques dealt with in this book. Because each style has its own terminology and because even commonly executed actions have no standardized names, the number of Indonesian words required would become an unwieldy burden on the reader who does not speak Indonesian.

Weapons

One of the unique features of pentjak-silat is its recognition of the importance of the various weapons available to the fighter and its freedom in permitting him to choose whichever seems most suitable to the particular occasion. By making correct use of the weapon he has chosen, the pentjak-silat exponent shapes the attacks of his enemy (or enemies), rendering them harmless, even if only momentarily, until a conclusive counterattack can be delivered. Knowledge of the nature of the various weapons available enables the fighter to deal effectively with the one chosen by his enemy.

Weapons used in pentjak-training and in silat-applications are of two chief types: anatomical (empty-hand or unarmed responses, making use of parts of the body); and implemental (armed responses, making use of tools as well as weapons). Customarily, training is first devoted to basic drills utilizing only anatomical weapons, and not until the trainee is adequately skilled in their application does he progress to other types of weapons. The shift from one type of weapon to the other involves no great change in posture or movement, for pentjak-silat anticipates the possible use of implemental weapons, and all empty-hand movements when correctly performed may, with equal effectiveness and safety, be used with implemental weapons. Let us consider, first, some of the anatomical weapons available. The choice of the part of the body to be used is very much as in *karate-dō*, but the formation of the weapon is not necessarily quite the same, nor is the choice of target area. A pentjak-silat exponent concentrates on the so-called center-line vital areas, regarding the most vulnerable part of the enemy's body as falling within an imaginary band looped around the longitudinal plane from the top of the head to the base of the groin; the width of this imaginary band is equivalent to the width of the enemy's head (see Figure 1).

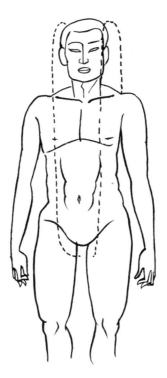

Fig. 1. The centerline vital areas

Fig. 2. HAND FORMATIONS

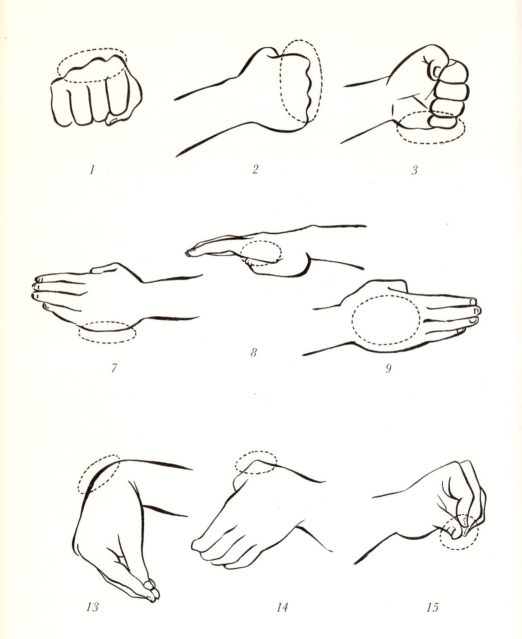

1 2 3

7 8 9

13 14 15

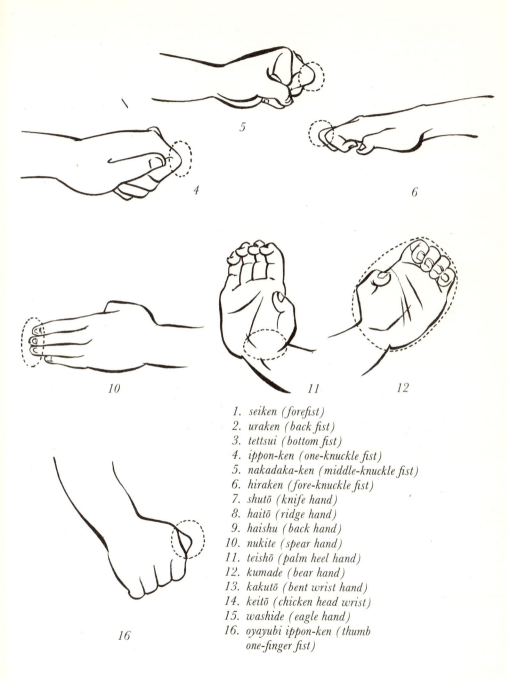

1. *seiken (forefist)*
2. *uraken (back fist)*
3. *tettsui (bottom fist)*
4. *ippon-ken (one-knuckle fist)*
5. *nakadaka-ken (middle-knuckle fist)*
6. *hiraken (fore-knuckle fist)*
7. *shutō (knife hand)*
8. *haitō (ridge hand)*
9. *haishu (back hand)*
10. *nukite (spear hand)*
11. *teishō (palm heel hand)*
12. *kumade (bear hand)*
13. *kakutō (bent wrist hand)*
14. *keitō (chicken head wrist)*
15. *washide (eagle hand)*
16. *oyayubi ippon-ken (thumb one-finger fist)*

A. THE HANDS

These may be formed in a great variety of ways for use in combat. Figure 2 depicts the formations of the hand that are so familiar in *karate-dō* they are not given explanatory descriptions here. However, pentjak-silat makes use of still other hand formations that are much less common, or wholly unknown, in *karate-dō*; these are shown in Figures 3 to 12 along with suggested methods of delivery and the most suitable target areas.

1. *The Arrowhead Fist:* In general formation, this hand weapon resembles the "forefist" (*seiken* of *karate-dō*), but there are some distinctions worth noting. The tight fist is held so that it is flexed and locked at the wrist, with the mid-knuckles in line with the long axis of the forearm, to form a concave or saddle-back sway on the back surface of the hand. Occasionally a convex surface is formed by flexion in the inward direction so as to reach certain targets (Figs. 3 and 4). Delivery of the arrowhead fist may be either by thrust or strike action. Favorite targets for the delivery of the arrowhead fist by either action include the face, throat, solar plexus, ribs, kidney areas, groin, the head, forearms, backs of hands, and shin-bones. Delivery of the arrowhead fist as a thrust punch into the midsection, throat, or face is shown in Training Exercise 9 (page 88).

Figs. 3—4. The Arrowhead Fist

22

2. *The Upright Fist:* The upright or standing fist (*tate-ken* of
karate-dō) is a tight fist flexed inward
and upward so that the main surface
of the fist contacts the target with
the two knuckles of the little finger
and the fourth finger (Fig. 5).
Valuable in upward hooking, side
hooking, and rising thrust punches,
this hand formation may be used
with great effect against both midsection and groin (shown in Training Exercise 15, page 104).

Fig. 5. The Upright Fist

3. *The Beak Hand:* The eagle
hand or the bent wrist (*washide* or
kakutō or *koken* of *karate-dō*) resembles
this widely used pentjak-silat hand
formation. Bring the tips of the
fingers and the thumb together,
holding them firmly under tension
by pressure so that you feel them to
be a unit. Flex your wrist, holding
your hand bent downward, at a bit

Fig. 6. The Beak Hand

less than its maximum extent. This formation should re-
semble, as its name indicates, the beak of a bird (Fig. 6).
The fingertips may be used in combination as a striking
surface; or the underside of the hand may be used to cup-
strike targets such as sensitive facial areas or the groin when
the target is "round the corner"—when the enemy is standing, say, with his back and left side to you and you want to
strike his right ear. By far the most important use of the beak
hand, however, is its function as a hook to catch the enemy
before hurling him off-balance. This is done by applying the
beak hand to the far side of his neck from behind or alongside and then swinging him circularly backward to the
ground as in Training Exercise 13–A (page 98).

4. *The Spearpoint Knuckle:* The middle-finger knuckle fist (*nakada-ka-ken*) of *karate-dō* resembles this way of shaping the hand. As is shown in Figure 7, the projecting middle finger must be tightly squeezed between the supporting ring finger on one side and the forefinger on the other; further, the inner tip of the thumb must press hard up and under the terminal row bone phalange of the middle finger. Held in this fashion, the middle finger will not, even under hard impact, slip back in line with the other fingers. The formation is used for both thrust and strike actions against vulnerable points, such as the temple, the back of the hand, the eyes, and other facial areas.

Fig. 7. The Spearpoint Knuckle

5. *The Buried Thumb Fist:* Somewhere between the chicken-head wrist and the thumb one-finger fist (*keitō* and *oyayubi ippon-ken*) of *karate-dō*, this hand weapon requires that the fist be tightly clenched on the thumb, as may be seen in Figure 8. The base of the knuckle of the thumb becomes the striking surface, and is effective against the sides of the enemy's neck, his temples, ribs, and kidney areas, when used in roundhouse or hooking punch fashion.

Fig. 8. The Buried Thumb Fist

24

6. *The Tiger's Claw Hand:* This particular formation is lacking in *karate-dō*, since scratching or raking is not permitted in sport organizations; it can be found in *karate-jutsu* forms. The hand is formed by holding the fingers and thumbs apart and flexing the tips; then the hand is tensed as though the fighter were trying to widen the distance between the thumb and the little finger. It is a weapon used primarily for raking or scratching the face, throat, or groin of the enemy. For its use, the reader is referred to Training Exercises 8–I (page 87) and 9–A (page 89).

Fig. 9. *The Tiger's Claw Hand*

7. *The Crane Fist:* This particular hand formation is less open in pentjak-silat than its counterparts in *karate-dō* (knuckle fist or bear hand, *hiraken* or *kumade*) or *ch'uan-fa*. As Figure 10 shows, the fighter bends his fingers inward but not so far as to allow the tips to touch the palm; the thumb also is bent and held apart from either the palm or the index finger; then the entire hand is firmly tensed. It may be delivered in either thrust or striking fashion at facial, head, rib, or groin targets. See Combat Situations, Baru pentjak-silat, Situation 1–B (page 124) or Setia Hati pentjak-silat, Situation 3–B (page 135).

Fig. 10. *The Crane Fist*

25

8. *The Reinforced Open Hand*: This is chiefly a blocking action and the *awase uke* of *karate-dō* resembles it. Both hands are open, and the hand that comes into direct contact with the enemy as a blocking surface uses its under or knife-edge surface for the purpose, while it is reinforced by the other hand, which covers it, and the palm of the other hand presses down against it (Fig. 11). See Combat Situations, Patai pentjak-silat, Situation 3–B (page 121). Another useful variation is that of the two hands working in concert but without touching each other. See Combat Situations, Tjimande pentjak-silat, 1 (page 126) and Training Exercises 11 and 12 (pages 95 and 96).

Fig. 11. The Reinforced Open Hand

9. *The Inverted Reverse Fist*: The downward hooking block (*gedan-kake-uke*) of *karate-dō* is similar in formation and delivery, but there are certain differences. It is best applied in retreat before an enemy's kicking attack. The open hand, with the little finger edge of the hand upward, is swung from the operator's outside in toward his centerline. Just before contact, and keeping the little finger uppermost, the hand is clenched into a tight fist, and the knuckles then contact the target. See Combat Situations, Patai pentjak-silat, Situation 3–A (page 121).

Fig. 12. The Inverted Reverse Fist

26

Some pentjak-silat exponents toughen their hands by holding them in various formations and pounding them against sand, wood, tile, and other materials. This toughening process is not overemphasized, however, as it often is in certain *karate-dō* styles. The reasons are fairly obvious. For one thing, most pentjak-silat exponents are laborers (tea pickers, rice farmers, loggers, fishermen, sailors) who, by virtue of their work, tend to have far stronger and tougher hands than the ordinary man; they have no special need of toughening-up exercises. Second, it will be found that when pentjak-silat techniques are properly delivered to scientifically chosen points of the anatomy, the normal hand is quite tough enough; it packs sufficient power to subdue the enemy; the pulverizing, destructive force so often acclaimed by *karate-dō* enthusiasts adds nothing.

B. THE ARMS

In pentjak-silat, as in *karate-dō*, the forearms are extremely useful weapons for blocking or parrying actions. Formation and delivery are, in fact, so highly similar in thesé two combative arts (in Korean and Okinawan arts too), that there is no necessity here for any lengthy and detailed explanation of the use of the forearms in pentjak-silat. A few differences may, however, be noted. Occasionally, in pentjak-silat, the forearms are used to deliver a direct blow in the attack. Topside, underside, and both inside and outside edges of the forearm may come into play, depending on the nature of the action. A Mustika Kwitang expert (page 28, ♯ 1–♯ 2) generates enough force to smash a coconut or a stack of five construction bricks with one blow of his foream. The Perisai Diri expert (♯ 3) can also strike with his forearm with equal skill and force, although he prefers to use the open hand.

Full-arm extensions in thrust or strike punches are less commonly used in pentjak-silat than in *karate-dō*. Probably experience has taught the dangers of full-arm extension and the advantages of stopping before the arm is fully extended.

The elbow is formed and used exactly as in *karate-dō* and therefore requires no elaboration here. It is a weapon for close infighting situations and can deliver an extremely powerful blow when correctly used. The reader is referred to Training Exercise 12 (page 96) and Combat Situations, Baru pentjak-silat, Situation 1–B (page 124) for examples of the use of the elbow.

The shoulder is commonly used as a point of contact against the enemy's midsection, ribs, lower back, thigh or groin; it serves, in every case, as the point of impact on the target, transmitting the power generated by both the posture and the movement of the fighter. Often the force of a shoulder blow is intended merely to topple the enemy rather than to serve as a knockout. For an example, see Training Exercise 10 (page 94).

C. THE HIPS AND BUTTOCKS

In utilizing the various hand formations available, as well as the arms, the exponent of pentjak-silat is far less dependent on hip rotation and thrust than is the *karate-dō* trainee. One reason is that more often than not pentjak-silat is carried out

28

under natural combative conditions—that is to say, on natural and uneven terrain, where forceful hip rotation may be detrimental to balance or even impossible to carry out. Hip rotation is based on stance, on feet strongly implanted on a level surface or one which affords purchase to the feet; when this sort of surface is lacking, hip rotation must naturally become less important. Further, many pentjak-silat tactics, such as may be seen, for example, in the Sumatran styles, use hip-checking actions which inhibit hip rotation and thrust, or negate altogether any dependence on them.

Pentjak-silat does, however, make free use of butting actions that involve the hips and buttocks as contact points, directing these weapons against the midsection, back, or thigh areas of the enemy. These tactics are commonly used in close infighting and grappling. For an example, see Combat Situations, Baru pentjak-silat, Situation 1–A (page 122).

D. THE FEET AND LEGS

After years of walking and running—and even of carrying heavy loads—over extremely harsh surfaces, like coral and volcanic sand or rocks, the soles of Indonesians' feet are so calloused they can produce abrasions on the skin by a mere grazing contact. No less amazing, and caused in large measure by the same active life, is the extreme flexibility and strength of the legs of the average Indonesian. Pentjak-silat exponents, not surprisingly, use to the fullest these qualities of both foot and leg.

They utilize all methods of kicking and kneeing currently in vogue with *karate-dō* enthusiasts, and the formation of the weapons and the methods of delivery are substantially the same, save that pentjak-silat makes greater use of the heel as a contact surface than does *karate-dō*; in this respect it is more closely allied to Chinese *ch'uan-fa* forms. The heel is perhaps most effective in thrusting types of kicks, although it can also be applied in forward snap-kicking fashion. For this, see Training Exercises 9–B and 9–C (pages 91–2).

The straight high kick of *ch'uan-fa* (a straight-legged high swing, as in punting a ball) is also widely used in pentjak-silat, as shown in Training Exercise 8–D (page 80). But probably most popular of all with pentjak-silat exponents is the leg sickle, which may be delivered in a frontal or reverse manner and which may be used either to hook-reap-sweep an enemy off his feet or merely to kick him. As a frontal leg sickle action, the leg is swung in roundhouse fashion from a low crouching posture or from a ground position, whereupon the ball or tip of the foot may serve to inflict pain by kicking into the target (head, neck, midsection, ribs, groin, knee), or the instep may be applied outside of and from behind the enemy's leg in an attempt to cut his foot out from under him. Examples of this action may be seen in Training Exercises 4 and 5 (pages 68 and 70); Harimau pentjak-silat, Situations 3 and 4 (pages 112 and 114); Setia Hati pentjak-silat, Situation 2 (page 133).

In the reverse sickle heel-kick action, the leg may be swung in reverse roundhouse fashion either to apply the back surface of the leg (below the knee) to the enemy's outside-rear leg, so as to cut the leg from under him, or to kick the heel into targets such as the head, midsection, ribs, groin, or knee. The action is shown in Training Exercises 6 and 7 (pages 72 and 74); Harimau pentjak-silat, Situations 1, 2, and 5 (pages 108, 110, and 116); and Perisai Diri pentjak-silat, Situation 1 (page 138).

E.   THE HEAD

Pentjak-silat, like Chinese, Korean, and other realistic fighting methods that originated on the Asian mainland, makes good use of the head for butting or thrusting actions. Head-on, side, and rear actions are effective in infighting situations, either to subdue the enemy or to set him up for some final measure.

Unlike orthodox *karate-dō*, pentjak-silat makes use of an extremely wide range of implemental weapons of various sorts, as do orthodox Chinese, Korean, and Okinawan combative arts, all of them thus taking on a quality of realism that is lacking in solely empty-hand combative forms.

Although it is beyond the scope of this book to describe all the possible weapons in detail, an account of some of them is indeed necessary for the exponent of pentjak-silat.

A. BLADE

The blade, being the favorite type of weapon used by Indonesians, is also, naturally enough, the favorite in pentjak-silat. Weapons of this type are numerous. A few of the most common are the *pedang*, a long, swordlike weapon, single-edged and somewhat akin to a cutlass or saber; the *parang* (Fig. 13), a shorter, single-edged weapon not unlike the machete; the *kris* (Fig. 14), a unique blade indigenous to Indonesia; and the *tombak*, a spear used throughout Indonesia.

B. STICK AND STAFF

The chief weapons of this type are the *tongkat* and the *gada*, which are short sticks, and the *gala* and the *toya*, which can vary in length from five to about seven feet. The wood out of which the sticks and staffs are most commonly fashioned is that of the rattan palm (called *roton* in Indonesian), although hard woods are also utilized.

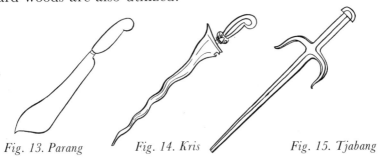

Fig. 13. Parang   *Fig. 14. Kris*   *Fig. 15. Tjabang*

C. FLAIL

Here would be included both chains (*rante*) and whips (the *chemeti* and the *penjut*). Chains in use show a great diversity of linkage patterns and overall length, both of which are, of course, determined by the user; the ends of the chain are usually weighted. As a weapon, the chain is chiefly used to beat the enemy, but it may also serve to entangle him and whatever weapon he happens to be wielding. The *chemeti* is the longer of the two types of whips.

D. PROJECTILE

The most important members of this family of weapons in Indonesia are the bow and arrow (*panah* and *anak panah*) and the blowpipe (*sumpit*). Their diversity and ingenuity of design are truly astonishing. Although not used for infighting, the stances and postures adopted in using this sort of weapon are modeled on the penjak-silat training and exercises. The projectile category also includes weapons which can be thrown as well as used in hand-to-hand combat. A good example is the spear (*tombuk*), which is customarily used in a fencing type of action but which obviously may also be utilized for hurling. The *piau* (a small knife for throwing) has many varieties throughout the country, and there are also weapons of the boomerang type as well as plain throwing sticks.

E. COMPOSITE

Weapons in this category may be used with equal facility for a wide variety of actions. One such is the *tjabang* (Fig. 15), an ancient Indonesian weapon of the truncheon type. It is made of iron and has double tines fastened at the juncture of shaft and handle.

The pentjak-silat exponent is never, in fact, "empty-handed", for almost any object within his reach such as a chair, a bottle, or a stone, may become a weapon of expediency in an emergency.

Techniques against Armed Attacks

In studying orthodox pentjak-silat, the trainee must sooner or later take into serious consideration how to cope with an armed assailant. He must, whether under conditions of training or in actual combat, learn the capabilities and limitations of an armed enemy. This he must do both when he is unarmed and when he is armed. (The latter, it must be noted, is beyond the scope of this book.)

The stress on combative reality cannot be overemphasized when the trainee is practicing the methods and exercises of pentjak-silat. He must do nothing in his training routine that he would not do in fighting an enemy who is trying to kill him. By concentrating on this in training he will be able to adapt the methods he has learnt with complete facility when a real combat situation occurs.

How well or rather how safely the trainee effects the outcome in dealing with an armed enemy is entirely dependent upon his understanding and abilities in meeting an unarmed enemy. If he can do that well, the transition to coping with the armed enemy is only a matter of application. The reader may gain a clearer understanding of this transition through the following illustrations of Tjingrik pentjak-silat.

TJINGRIK
PENTJAK-SILAT

METHOD A

In #1, the assailant (on right) is standing with his left side
to the camera, and his right hand, though empty for the
purpose of the illustration, could easily be holding a weapon
with which to strike at the defender, whose responses may
well be the same whether the hand is empty or not. Two
methods of defense will illustrate this point.

The defender has already, in # 1, intercepted the assailant's right arm with a sweeping open-handed catch of that
arm from the inside, using his left hand to grasp the attacking
arm between the elbow and the wrist. Following Method A,
the defender pulls the assailant's attacking arm forward and
downward, thus jerking him off-balance and forwards. The
defender simultaneously strikes with his opened right hand,
using a knife-edged formation, at the assailant's head (# 2).
The assailant's reaction to this blow is one of shock as he, at

the same time, attempts to resist the forward movement imposed on him by the defender. This he does by straightening his body and leaning backward, putting himself off-balance backwards. Even had the defender's intended blow fallen short, the combined action would have had the all-important effect of moving the assailant back. The defender utilizes this reaction of the assailant to throw him backwards to the ground. He does so by putting his right leg behind the assailant's right leg and, using the combined power of both his arms, forces the assailant further backward over the outstretched leg (# 3). Note that the defender does not step forward until he has obtained a rearward movement from his enemy. This is a safeguard: if the assailant does not react by moving backward, the defender is still in a position to deliver a forward snap-kick into the groin of his enemy.

METHOD B

Method B is shown above (♯ 1–♯ 3). In the first two, the defender has used a left-hand catch on the assailant's attacking right arm in order to "float" the assailant upward and forward by pulling the captured arm toward him on a plane more or less parallel to that of the ground. Simultaneously, he has taken two other actions; he has put his right foot just in front of his assailant's right foot, and he is in the process of delivering an open-handed knife-edge blow to the left side of his assailant's head or neck. In ♯ 3, he uses the combined power of his arms and a sharp twist of his body to the left in order to wheel the assailant backward to the ground. Note that in Method B the defender steps forward immedi-

ately, at the moment that he pulls the assailant forward and delivers his open-handed blow. To have remained behind would have invited a kick from the enemy, perhaps with devastating results for the defender.

Once the defender's response to the unarmed assailant has been perfected in both methods, a weapon may be placed in the assailant's right hand and identical responses to the attacks shown practiced. Under these conditions the the addition of certain weapons changes nothing in the mechanics of defense—but does serve to heighten the emotional atmosphere of the combat.

METHOD A

Tactics of Pamur pentjak-silat exponents on the island of
Madura, in dealing with an overhead slashing knife attack,
show a remarkable similarity to the Tjingrik methods just
described. In # 1 the assailant, wielding a knife (*todi*) in his
right hand, has been intercepted by an open left-handed
catch on his right wrist; the defender has also put his right
leg behind that of the assailant. Without using a striking
action, the defender has secured his right hand under the
left armpit of the assailant. He then wheels the assailant
backward to the ground by the combined use of both his

38

arms and a sharp twist of his body to the left (♯ 2). An interesting method of controlling the assailant is illustrated in ♯ 3. As the assailant hits the ground in front of the standing defender, the latter keeps control of the knife arm with both hands as he stamps his left heel or foot-edge into the head of the fallen enemy. (This latter action is symbolized in the photograph by the juxtaposition of head and heel.) By pressing his foot on the enemy's head or by repeatedly stamping on it, the defender can force the knife out of the enemy's hand and so gain control of the situation.

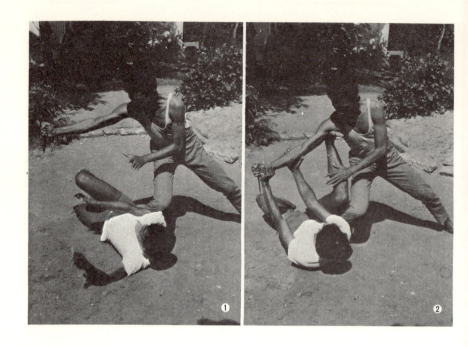

METHOD B

Exponents of the Pamur style have developed a tactic designed to counter the failure of the tactics described above and to enable the defender to regain his lost advantage. The attempt to throw the knife-wielding assailant has failed, and # 1 shows how the latter has been able to throw the defender to the ground instead. The assailant has reversed the position of his knife, a tactic at which Madurese fighters are highly skilled, and is now about to strike it downward at the apparently prostrate defender. The latter, however, has a tactic at his disposal by means of which he will regain control of the situation: he quickly rams his right foot, sole flat, into the assailant's armpit and at the same time grabs hold with both hands of the assailant's knife-wielding right arm (# 2). Note in this figure that the knuckles of the defender's left hand face upward and those of his right hand face down-

40

ward. The pressure, upward with the right hand and downward with the left, with the right foot still jammed into the assailant's arm, will be very painful to him. The defender, however, has further action in mind which requires very careful timing and synchronization. He slides his right hand down the assailant's captured right arm (# 3) and at the same time rolls quickly toward his left with a violent upward thrust of his right foot. His hands snap downward. The assailant attempts to save himself a nasty fall by stretching out his left arm; the knife he is still holding in his captured right arm can, however, only prove a source of danger to him, and he drops the blade as he falls out of fear of cutting himself (# 4). The defender, now that the assailant is unarmed and on the ground, can snatch the blade himself and take whatever steps are necessary to subdue his enemy.

41

Mustika Kwitang
Pentjak-silat

METHOD A

The Mustika Kwitang style also offers unarmed defense against a knife-bearing (*pisau belati*) enemy. Two different methods of defense are illustrated here; both begin with ♯ 1, where the defender (on the left side) is confronted by an assailant holding a knife in his right hand. The first method of defense is shown in ♯ 2 to ♯ 4. In the first of these, the assailant has lunged deeply forward in an attempt to thrust his knife into the belly of the defender, who has evaded the thrust by adroitly shifting his body to the outside of the knife-wielding arm. Simultaneously, his right hand catches hold of the attacking wrist, his palm covering the back of the hand, his thumb pointing downward. He then pulls the captured arm across his right thigh toward his hip, rotating the arm to bring it elbow upward. The knife-wielding arm

42

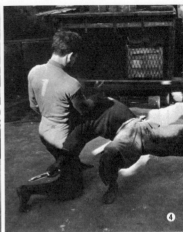

is now securely wedged between the defender's thigh and upper body. At the same time, the defender strikes the assailant's captured elbow with a hard downward blow of his left wrist-forearm; the force must break or otherwise severely injure the joint. With the attacking arm now rendered useless, the defender, while keeping it pinned against thigh and body, releases his right hand to deliver a hard upright fist directly into his assailant's face or side of head, and with his left hand he grips the enemy's hair (# 3). Twisting his body to the left and using his left hand to pull his assailant's head, the defender wheels the assailant over onto his back and then completes the subduing action by striking his knife-edged right hand against the throat of the enemy (# 4).

METHOD B

The second method of defense, illustrated in #1 to #5, is even more dynamic. Once again, the assailant armed with a knife in his right hand confronts an unarmed defender. In #2, the upraised left arm of the assailant is met by the defender's right arm, since there is always the possibility that the knife has been switched; but in #3 the assailant makes his lunge, with the knife in his right hand, toward the belly of the defender. The latter evades the attack by shifting his body to the left, and simultaneously renders the

44

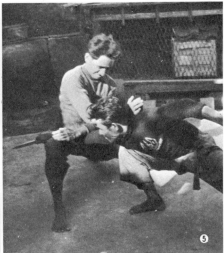

attacking arm helpless by an open-hand interception along
the top-inside of the assailant's forearm and by downward
and inward pressure of his hand, forcing the arm between
his thigh and abdomen (# 4). The defender does not let the
fact that his right arm is still raised go to waste; using his
wrist-forearm area as the contact point, he brings that arm
down hard, in a striking action, against the cervical region
of the assailant's spine. The result is that the armed enemy is
knocked unconscious (# 5).

45

METHOD C

Another Mustika Kwitang technique to combat attack by an enemy armed with a knife is illustrated here in the sequence shown in ♯ 1 to ♯ 10. In ♯ 1, it is evident that the assailant has positioned his knife for an overhead downward thrusting attack and is crouched ready to spring. When he makes the attack, the defender moves forward to meet him and arrests the attacking arm while it is still in an upright position (♯ 2). It will be noted that the defender's left hand, held open, as it contacts the assailant's arm just above the elbow, presses up and in toward the assailant's head, while the palm of the right hand, also held open, is pressed against the underside of the attacker's forearm, near the wrist. ♯ 3 shows the process by means of which the defender gets conrol of the attacking arm. First he changes the grip of his left hand so that it cups the assailant's elbow, and then he stretches his right hand further around the top of the assailant's forearm. Once these grips have been accom-

46

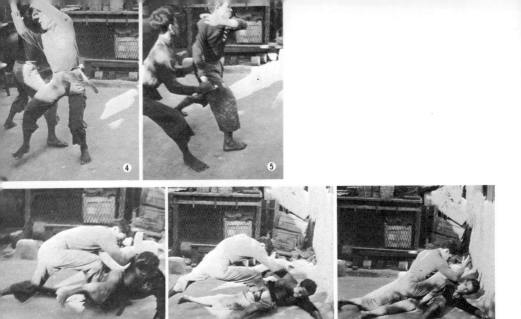

plished, the defender steps forward on his right leg and moves through to a position behind the assailant; simultaneously, he swings the enemy's captured right arm downward and up around to carry it in front of his forward movement. The defender now brings the assailant's arm to a new high position (♯ 4) and then ducks under it by pivoting on his right foot, the position of which he has just changed, and bringing his left foot in a short arc behind him; as he comes around to the back (and somewhat to the right) of the assailant, the defender pulls the captured arm down (♯ 5). He must now immediately work the arm up the assailant's back in a hammerlock (♯ 6 and ♯ 7). Releasing his left-hand grip, the defender pushes hard against his assailant's back, sending him sprawling to the ground; he must, during this portion of the action, keep up the hammerlock pressure (♯ 8 and ♯ 9). The defender completes the action with a right forearm strike to the head or neck of his enemy (♯ 10).

47

Basic Postures for Combat

Every specific style of pentjak-silat has its own technical characteristics, chief among which are the combative postures and movements. By observing the posture an enemy has assumed, and his subsequent movements, an expert can tell immediately what particular style of pentjak-silat he is up against, what attacks and defenses he may expect, and what defenses and countermeasures may be most safely and effectively used in coping with the enemy.

To categorize all the various combative postures pentjak-silat makes use of would be a herculean task, and one obviously beyond the bounds of an introductory book of this nature. However, there are certain typical combative postures that may—and indeed must—be recognized if the novice is to make any progress in acquiring skill in the art. He should study each as it is presented and learn to identify its essential technical characteristics; this, in turn, will give him invaluable clues as to its combative purpose and advantages.

In preparation for the emergencies of actual combat, pentjak-silat exponents make use of extremely varied and interesting training exercises. Above all, they presuppose a strong and flexible body—one capable of executing specific movements with speed, force, and precision. Because a pentjak-silat expert can go through his training exercises with such skill and grace, displaying a smooth delivery of action that is so subtly pleasing to the eye, many casual observers become convinced that what they are watching is in reality a dance form. Nothing could be further from the truth. Pentjak is preparatory training for actual combat.

Before taking up the all-important question of training exercises, however, some typical combative postures need to be described.

SUMATRA

All Sumatran pentjak-silat styles make extensive use of leg tactics. Due to the environment of the people who reside on this large island, fighting tactics have come to rely on well-developed leg flexibility and strength. These special qualities have been made possible by the daily exercise involved in labor chores that require full-squatting, climbing, and jumping actions. Whether a lowland, coastal, or mountain resident, a Sumatran pentjak-silat exponent demonstrates an unusual ability with leg maneuvers, but is not at a loss when the hands and arms must be brought into use.

1. HARIMAU PENTJAK-SILAT

The Menangkabau people of west-central Sumatra have made the Harimau ("tiger") style a very effective and dangerous fighting form that is respected throughout Indonesia. Its technical fundamentals can be found, to a greater or lesser degree, in every other major orthodox pentjak-silat style, but important reasons for differences arise from the fact that uneven and slippery ground surfaces are most common in Sumatra, and that under these conditions, the Harimau fighter considers an upright combative posture detrimental to effective fighting since it offers him only two bases of support—i.e., his legs. He prefers to hug the ground, sometimes actually getting down on it, thus making effective use of five supports—his two legs, his two arms, and either his back, side, or belly. To assume that, while in this unusual recumbent posture, the Harimau fighter is incapable of moving quickly and effectively would be to make a gross— and possibly dangerous—mistake. From the low posture he assumes, he can deliver very powerful kicks as well as make use of other cunning tactics; further, he can spring quickly and forcefully up at the enemy, clawing him with terrifying ferocity.

2. KUMANGO PENTJAK-SILAT

Since this fighting form developed along sandy beach areas, it prefers an upright posture and has shaped its tactics to terrain with a loose topsoil where ordinary speed of operation is hampered. It has influenced a few other major styles, all of them Sumatran. Kumango is, on the whole, a well-balanced system, using both arm and leg tactics, but quite often the arms serve only to distract the enemy. This may be done by extending one arm and slapping the other resoundingly against the thigh, or it may be accomplished by means of throwing sand. Skillful footwork combines with real and simulated kicking actions to make frontal positioning against a Kumango fighter very dangerous. The characteristic combative posture of Kumango can, when combined with its rhythmic movements, tend to lull the enemy into a feeling of false security.

3. PATAI
PENTJAK-SILAT

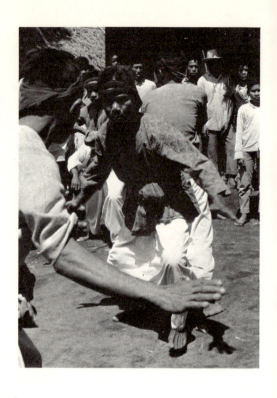

Evolved in the mountainous Bukittinggi region of Sumatra, this is one of the most rhythmic of all styles. Its dancelike motion suggests less than maximum combative effectiveness, and its postures actually seem to invite attack, especially kicking attacks. Efficient hand blocking and parrying actions, however, worked from low crouching levels, render all but the cleverest kicks harmless; this is partly the result of the fact that the Patai fighter will always try to station himself on higher terrain than is occupied by his enemy. All combative postures may serve as bases for kicking actions, but Patai makes another characteristic use of the legs. This is the employment of the foot to block or parry the attack of an enemy, especially if he is armed.

4. BARU PENTJAK-SILAT

This is a relatively new style that comes from the coastal Padang area. It achieves a balance between arm and leg techniques, making use of combative postures adapted to all types of terrain. As its chief preference, however, seems to be for grappling tactics, the exponent of the Baru style depends on secure footholds. He likes to dig his feet into the soil, and does so from static postures so that this is not noticed by the enemy. From these braced footholds, the Baru fighter moves with speed and power before the enemy can mount his attack.

JAVA

Javanese systems of pentjak-silat tend to make a balanced use of the body, although most combative postures seem to suggest that fighters prefer hand and arm tactics and choose postures from which these tactics may be instantly applied; postures of the orthodox styles are very varied, ranging from the upright to the low crouch. Javanese fighters use both the open and closed hand with equal facility. In addition to tactics of the usual striking variety, they are capable also of grappling actions executed from close infighting situations. Javanese pentjak-silat exponents are extremely supple and lithe—a fact that probably accounts for the characteristically soft and willowlike movements produced by changing combative postures.

1.   TJIMANDE PENTJAK-SILAT

Though developed in the wet lowlands, this fighting form is now confined almost exclusively to the Sundanese people of west Java, a rural, mountainous region. Tjimande postures are less upright than those of other Javanese pentjak-silat systems, and movements are made cautiously, as though the fighter were trying to avoid wet and slippery spots on the ground. The flexibility that Tjimande combative postures permit is ideally suited to meet an enemy who rushes in hard to the attack. Through clever use of hand- and arm-parrying actions, the Tjimande fighter meets the initial attack, then neutralizes it by further covering action, and finally—and virtually simultaneously—delivers his counterattack.

54

2. MUSTIKA KWITANG PENTJAK-SILAT

Also to be found in west Java, but centering around the metropolitan Djakarta area, this dynamic method of fighting is an extremely powerful system that is not content with mere evasive actions, no matter how clever they may be. It dedicates all the forces of the body to the fury of a counter-attack, and from its dramatic combative postures derives the explosive force that, when fully released, will subdue most enemies. This system of pentjak-silat achieves a good balance between arm and leg tactics; although it may perhaps favor the former, it is realistic enough to prepare for an enemy who fights primarily with his feet, and it can retaliate in the same manner. By working at the task of toughening both hands and feet, the Mustika Kwitang exponent can generate enough power to smash a coconut with one blow—and he can apply a similar force with great accuracy against his enemy's vital regions.

3. Tjingrik
Pentjak-silat

Inasmuch as the wild monkey of west Java has inspired this particular style of fighting, it seeks to imitate that animal in combat and is essentially, therefore, an arm and hand system. To this it adds certain unique combative postures. As might be expected, the system is highly acrobatic and seeks to baffle the enemy by surprise attack and speed of movement. The Tjingrik exponent is able to leap full-length at an upright enemy from a position of sitting on the ground. His two chief targets are the throat and groin, and he will claw at these viciously, attempt to tear them apart with his open hands, and even bite them.

56

4. SETIA HATI PENTJAK-SILAT

This system, based essentially on leg tactics, arose in central Java. Its combative postures are designed to make the enemy expect retaliation by hands and arms and be unaware of the imminence of a powerful kick. The Setia Hati exponent will pretend to slip quietly away from his assailant and to be willing to accept defeat; then suddenly he will surprise his overconfident enemy with well-directed and powerful kicking actions. From any position, either upright or on the ground, the Setia Hati fighter is a dangerous enemy.

5. PERISAI DIRI PENTJAK-SILAT

This east Javan fighting form is the most staccato in rhythm of all pentjak-silat styles. Its abrupt movements are made possible by exceptionally upright combative postures which constitute a large part of its wide range of tactics. Perisai Diri is essentially a hand and arm system, which, when combined with its upright combative postures, provides some of the cleverest and most effective defenses known to man. The Perisai Diri fighter does not exclude leg tactics but the ones he chooses have their technical roots deep in Sumatran pentjak-silat. Making use of combative postures selected from both human and animal positions, Perisai Diri exponents exhibit a speed of hand and arm movements second to none.

MADURA

On the island of Madura, the pentjak-silat fighter is usually either a sailor or a farmer with a volatile temper. He has borrowed what he liked from other pentjak-silat styles, and has achieved good balance between arm, leg, and grappling tactics. His combative postures, thus, are quite variable and tend to make an encounter with a Madurese fighter a difficult and dangerous proposition. This fact is recognized by Indonesian peoples, most of whom genuinely fear him.

PAMUR PENTJAK-SILAT

This, the major orthodox style of Madura, has borrowed its tactics largely from the Riouw Archipelago and from the Menangkabau and Atjeh peoples of Sumatra. The Pamur stylist deftly evades attack and at the same time delivers a powerful countermeasure. He relies a lot on misdirecting the attacker's energy and then catching the attacking arm or leg so as to render it harmless before he counterattacks. The ardor of the Madurese Pamur fighter combines with his physical fitness to keep his fearsome reputation unblemished.

BALI

The reputation of the people of Bali—that they are unaggressive and shy—appears to be well founded; they are reluctant to be prodded into the state of mind that is essential to a fight, yet once they are aroused, their ardor is equal to that of any other racial group of Indonesians. Their combative postures are fierce, and their fighting is skillful, featuring a good balance between arm and leg tactics.

Bhakti Negara Pentjak-silat

Efficient fighting forms are the keynote of this style of combat, and all its exponents are skilled technicians, at home in an upright position or on the ground. Evasive action is covered by clever arm and hand tactics using both the open and the closed hand. Bhakti Negara fighters are also masters of cunning. Should an unsuspecting enemy grasp an arm that seemed to be inadvertently offered, he will be slapped—not to loosen the grip but rather to distract him long enough so that he will be unaware that the real countermeasure is already being applied.

Training Exercises

No training exercise described here is merely an isolated rehearsal in agility or clever movement; each is directly related to some particular fighting tactic. The reader is advised to pay special attention to the textual description of the exercise as well as to the illustrations, for sometimes the limitations of photography have cancelled the authors' efforts to record as faithfully as possible what was being enacted before the lens, and, in such cases, the written word must be relied on to impart information that the photographs fail to show.

Pentjak-silat begins, naturally enough, as we have already indicated, with empty-hand pentjak training exercises. The trainee should practice each exercise precisely and slowly until he begins to feel that he is gaining confidence in the technique. When he is satisfied that he is doing exactly what the text calls for, then he attempts to inject into his execution of the exercise first fluency and then speed. It is only constant repetition that will enable him to perform the exercise accurately, smoothly, and quickly. He must repeat each training exercise over and over again until it feels "comfortable"; any other feeling means that he is still short of his goal.

60

The student will find that many of the exercises given here are indispensible to correct performance of some of the combative actions described in the following chapter, but not all exercises are directly linked to the action shown there. Some have been given merely because they are obviously useful and may be easily converted to combat. In such cases, it is for the trainee to devise his own applications.

In any case, he must always bear in mind that the soft and silky, yet precise, movements of the pentjak-silat expert are the result of many hours of dedicated study and practice. A good share of the expert's training time is devoted to exercises, many of which appear in this chapter. Unless the trainee is prepared to devote himself with similar wholeheartedness to the training exercises, he cannot hope to master the combative tactics described in the chapter that follows.

TRAINING EXERCISE 1

This is an exercise in alertness, speed, balance, and agility. The Perisai Diri style of east Java uses it extensively to equip trainees with the ability to deal effectively with surprise attacks from behind or from the sides; it is ideal training also in learning how to handle more than one assailant. Perisai Diri exponents are particularly well known for their ability to change direction quickly and—through the use of such abrupt body changes—to move speedily and effectively into new lines of attack or defense.

METHOD A. Stand naturally, with your arms at your sides; your straddle stance reflects the fact that you are not expecting an attack (♯ 1). At a verbal signal (such as a shout) from a training partner, jump high into the air and, as you do, turn either to the right or to the left (a left turn is illustrated in ♯ 2), so that you land on your feet in any fighting posture that seems most suitable to you (♯ 3).

62

METHODS B AND C. You are already in a combative posture, as though engaged with an enemy. On signal, jump and turn so as to land in either the same combative posture (shifting to right or left if you desire) or an entirely different one, such as would be necessary if you were being attacked by another assailant. (♯ 4–♯ 5 and ♯ 6–♯ 8.)

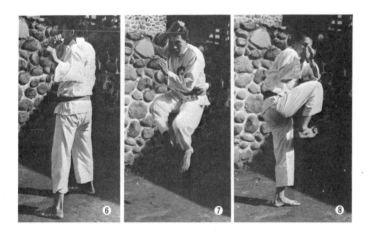

In this exercise, no matter which method you employ, your leap and turn while in the air must result in your facing a wholly new direction—that, in fact, of your new enemy (in this case, of course, your training partner). The trainee should practice turns of at least ninety degrees, and he will probably find it useful (as Indonesians do) to punctuate all jumps with a loud, intimidating shout.

TRAINING EXERCISE 2

A west-central Sumatran tactic of the Kumango style, this exercise is intended to develop a deceptive forward stepping action which may be instantly transformed into a forward straight-line snap kick. It is a tactic designed for use on sandy ground or terrain with a loose topsoil, where footing is precarious and movement less quick than on hard, flat ground. Variations of this technique may be used to force an enemy backwards.

METHOD. Assume a Kumango-style combative posture as you step forward with your right foot. Stretch your left arm out parallel to the ground, with the opened palm facing a bit forward and downward. Slap the inside of your upper right thigh with your right palm (♯1). If the enemy has closed in quickly, and if you are on natural terrain, drop quickly into a low crouch, scoop up loose earth or stones, and fling them into the enemy's face to drive him backward (♯2). This tactic may be omitted if it seems unnecessary. Now rise

immediately and bring your trailing left foot forward, slapping the upper part of your left thigh with your left palm; your right hand and arm are carried well forward, anticipating blocking or parrying requirements (♯ 3); fake a forward snap kick with your left leg before you actually put it down (♯ 4). Immediately begin taking another step forward with your right foot and carry your left arm out to your left side as before; again slap your upper right thigh with your right hand (♯ 5). As you place your right foot on the ground, quickly shift your weight onto it and deliver a forceful forward snap kick with your trailing left leg which now goes directly into the kick instead of making another fake kick or step (♯6 and ♯7). The Kumango sequence of forward step, fake kick, forward step, and then the actual kick, supposes that the enemy is retreating; the illustrations show the minimum movement, which can, of course, be lengthened to as many steps and fake kicks as may seem appropriate to the situation.

TRAINING EXERCISE 3

This leg and arm tactic of the Patai penjak-silat style from west-central Sumatra is an interesting one. It is an exercise designed to develop balance in the trainee and sensitivity to changes in the enemy's posture.

METHOD. You and your training partner are facing each other as you stand on your right legs; your left arms are engaged, with the hands open with the knife edges or wrists pressing against each other (♯ 1). Your raised left legs may be correspondingly engaged (not shown), with the outer ankle surfaces against each other. Either training partner may, without warning, change his stance, and the other must immediately respond by following suit, so that arms and perhaps legs are engaged as before (♯ 2). By pressure, pushing and pulling arm against arm and leg against leg, each partner tries to throw the other off-balance or make him lower his raised leg to the ground in order to

retain balance. At any time a partner may disengage his arm, using it to push or pull the other off-balance (although without grasping the other's garments), or he may choose to disengage his raised leg, either simultaneously with an arm movement or not, and set it on the ground—provided that by so doing he tumbles his partner or at least brings him down to one knee (♯ 3–♯ 4). The free arm may be used to pull or push only after the leg been lowered. Note that in ♯ 3, the training partner on the right side has disengaged and, after lowering his right foot to the ground, has shoved his right arm against the left side of his partner's chest. In ♯ 4, he has used his right leg as a pivot over which he topples his partner. The hand and arm actions of the "victor" are noteworthy: as his left wrist is held by his partner's left hand, he is tugging to extend that arm, and he has put his right arm under the left arm of his downed partner. He completes his toppling action by flinging his right arm upward and to the right front (♯ 5).

TRAINING EXERCISE 4

The Setia Hati style of central Java lays the greatest emphasis on combative leg actions. The exercise given here provides useful training in balance as well as in the ability to deliver a kick from the ground, a posture that might be the result of intentional positioning or accidental slipping or being knocked down by an enemy.

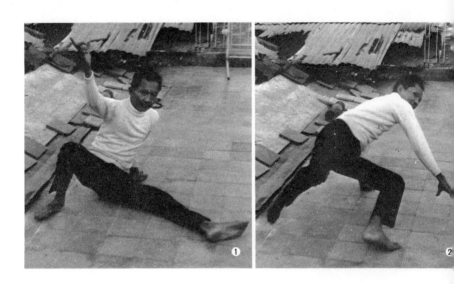

METHOD A. From the ground posture shown in ♯ 1, swing your right leg in roundhouse kick fashion, high enough to strike the groin or midsection of an enemy who has closed in on you. Continue the kick so that it revolves your whole body, as shown in ♯ 2 and ♯ 3. Rise to your feet with a complete revolution of your body, first putting your weight on your right leg and letting your left leg "float" (♯ 4), then quickly shift your weight onto your left leg and deliver a forward snap kick with your right foot (♯ 5).

METHOD B. From the same ground posture (♯ 1) and the initial action (♯ 2), the roundhouse kick can be made intentionally unsuccessful, so as to fool the enemy and avoid his attack. Then, with both your hands on the ground, spring into a right-hand combative posture (♯ 6–♯ 7).

The Harimau style of west-central Sumatra attempts to emulate the movements of the tiger from which it takes its name. The following exercise, basic to the Harimau style, has been designed to develop continuous and rapid alternate frontal leg sickle kicking abilities from a ground position.

METHOD. For the purpose of this exercise, your training partner, whom you face, is required to move backward in any natural or convenient manner; he must play a purely defensive role, blocking or avoiding your sickle kick actions; he should, however, try to stay as close in to you as is safe, so that he may learn to cope with this particular maneuver; and he may use his hands or evasive stepping actions to avoid being kicked. From a left stance (♯ 1), drop to the ground, supporting yourself on your left hand; hold your right hand out, palm toward your partner, to ward off possible aggressive actions (♯ 2). As you begin to bring your trailing right leg forward, place your right hand on the

ground for added support; then swing your right leg in roundhouse fashion, trying to strike your instep against the outside of your partner's forward leg (at the knee or below) with enough power to hook or reap his leg out from under him (# 3). Stabilizing your body now with both hands and using your bent left knee on the ground as a pivot, roll your body a bit to your left. Your aim is to deliver another kick with your left leg, similar to the one just described, to the other side of your partner's body. To do this, withdraw your right leg somewhat, planting it firmly on the ground in front of you and a bit to your left; twist your body to the right and place your right hand on the ground for support; as your weight shifts more onto your right hand and leg, swing your left leg in roundhouse kick fashion, rolling your body to the right and placing your left hand near your right for added support; your right knee now acts as the pivot (# 4–# 5). Force your partner backward in this manner as fast as you can. Learn not only to use your instep to hook but also the ball of your foot to kick against your partner's knee joint.

TRAINING EXERCISE 6

Among the leg tactics that the Perisai Diri style has borrowed from Sumatra is the reverse leg sickle action executed from the ground. The basic mechanics of this interesting and powerful skill may be learned from this exercise.

METHOD. Facing your training partner from a left combative posture, step forward onto your left foot, deeply to his left and behind him (# 1). Now quickly turn your body a bit to your left and drop onto your right knee, supporting yourself with both hands on the ground (# 2). Swing your extended left leg in an arc behind you, using a sickle motion against the

back of your partner's leg just above the ankle and below the calf (# 3). Continue the sickle action until you topple your partner to the ground; if the action has been correctly executed, he will fall backward (# 4). Sometimes he will contrive to keep his balance but at the same time will be so unstable as to allow you to stand quickly behind him and knee or kick him with your right leg in either the groin or the base of the spine (# 5). The entire action must be completed quickly. At first, the training partner submits to the action; later, he will try to remain on his feet. The initial position (# 1) may be voluntary or it may be the result of a slip; it is best taken when the enemy is in a left stance.

Training Exercise 7

Perisai Diri pentjak-silat exponents can deliver a reverse leg sickle heel kick with speed and efficiency. This exercise lays the foundation for that tactic.

METHOD. Assume a right stance, your right side quartering into your training partner (♯ 1). Step forward on your right foot (♯ 2), and, as you put your weight on it, bend forward from the waist and with your trailing left leg swing a reverse

sickle kick around behind you (# 3). Aim to place a heel kick into your training partner's groin or midsection (# 4). Your right hand should cover your groin as protection against counterattacks to that vital region; your left arm remains free, so that if you lose your balance or are knocked down, it will offer you support on the ground. As with Exercise 6, your training partner becomes more active as you acquire greater skill in the execution of the maneuver.

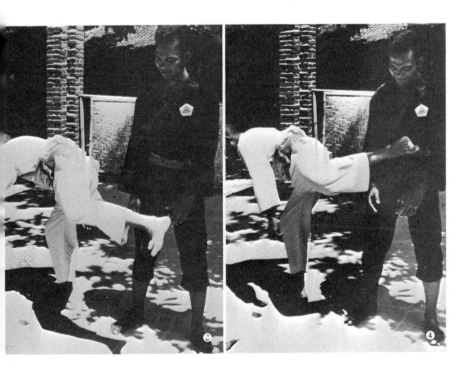

The posture of sitting on the ground is the most truly characteristic of pentjak-silat tactics; it is found in all major orthodox styles, although some have tended to minimize its use. Despite the variety of ways in which it may be employed, the basic factor, common to all styles, is that it is a deceptive tactic, a clever ruse by means of which you hope to lure your enemy into thinking he has found a momentary weakness in your defense. The following exercises allow the trainee to practice the basic forms of the posture of sitting on the ground and give some elementary applications as well. By means of the exercises, the trainee may develop a fine sense of balance, good judgment of distance, and unexpected strength and flexibility of leg and hip. The physical exertion involved in the exercises is valuable enough, but when they are correctly performed, smoothly and rapidly, they become the foundation for efficient fighting tactics. Four pentjak-silat styles have been studied to describe the mechanics of this ground posture, the importance of which cannot be overemphasized. As a preliminary remark to the methods given below, it should be noted that the posture has two aspects. One, called *depok*, results from the withdrawal of the forward leg of your combative posture and bringing it in front of your platform leg as you retreat from the enemy and lower your body to the ground; or you may advance, bringing your trailing leg forward but behind the leading leg of your combative posture as you lower yourself. The other aspect, the opposite process of leg positioning, is called *sempok*. Here you bring the leading leg behind your platform leg as you retreat and lower your body to the ground; or advancing, you bring the trailing leg forward and place it ahead of the leading leg as you lower your body. Both *depok* and *sempok* must be practiced until they can be performed with flexibility and power as you advance or retreat from both right and left combative postures.

METHOD A. The following exercise is used for *depok* training on the island of Madura; it is in the Pamur style. Stand in any combative posture (right posture is shown in # 1). Shift all your weight to your left leg and retreat from the enemy by bringing your advanced right leg back and in toward your platform left leg (# 2). Draw your right leg up by bending the knee so that you are standing on your left leg; maintain balance by means of your arms (# 3). Quickly bring your raised right leg in front of your platform left leg as you lower your body (# 4). Sit down on the ground, with your weight evenly distributed and your arms in protective position to block or parry (# 5). Rise quickly and smoothly by reversing the action and return to your original combative posture.

METHOD B. The Maduran Pamur style of *sempok* in this exercise begins, for the sake of simplicity, from a right combative posture (# 1). Retreat by withdrawing your advanced right leg and bringing it up to your platform left leg (# 2). Bend your right leg at the knee and bring it behind your left (# 3). Put your right foot down somewhat to the left and sink to the ground (# 4). You must sit with your weight evenly distributed. Rise by reversing these movements and return to your original combative posture.

METHOD C. The Madurese Pamur exponent executes the *depok* in retreat from his enemy by kicking as he rises. Assume the *depok* in Method A (# 1). Rise quickly (# 2); as your weight falls onto your left leg, twist to your right and swing your right leg forward into a frontal snap kick action; your platform foot pivots a bit toward the enemy, and your arms help to maintain balance as you kick (# 3).

METHOD D. The basic Madurese Pamur *sempok* exercise is also given an applicable meaning by means of a kick action. Begin from *sempok* as would be taken from a left combative posture (see sketch). Rise quickly (# 1); and, as your weight falls on your right leg, swing your left leg forward into a frontal high kick (# 2).

METHOD E. If the Madurese Pamur exponent is in a *sempok* (taken from the right combative posture shown), he can rise quickly and hold a new combative posture which threatens kicking by side thrust action (♯2–♯3).

METHOD F. Exponents of the Bhakti Negara style also come out of *sempok* posture in various ways. First, assume a *sempok*, taken from the left combative posture (♯ 1); then rise quickly until you attain the position shown in ♯ 6. At this point, according to the situation confronting you, you may do one of several things:

(a) kick directly forward with your withdrawn left leg in snap kick fashion or use a high kick (neither action is illustrated);

(b) step forward on your left foot and then quickly

82

deliver a forward snap kick with your right foot (♯ 7);
(c) step forward on your left leg and then quickly raise
your right leg in a new combative posture that offers
a threat to the enemy (♯ 8).

These three actions are, naturally, reversible; that is to say,
you may use them to go from a standing posture to the
sempok. In all actions, pay particular attention to protective
arm and hand actions.

METHOD G. The Bhakti Negara exponent will on occasion combine changes of combative posture and position with the *sempok*. First, assume any right combative posture (♯ 1). The next maneuver may take one of two forms: you may make a wide step directly your right with your right leg, swinging it in a short arc to your right rear (♯ 2), before going down into *sempok* (♯ 4–♯ 6); or you may pivot on your left leg (which is to the rear) and swing your right leg back 180° so that you assume a left combative posture (♯ 3) before going down into *sempok* (♯ 4–♯ 6). By reversing the actions, you come from *sempok* back to your original right combative posture (shown in ♯ 1). Here, too, special attention must be paid to arm and hand action.

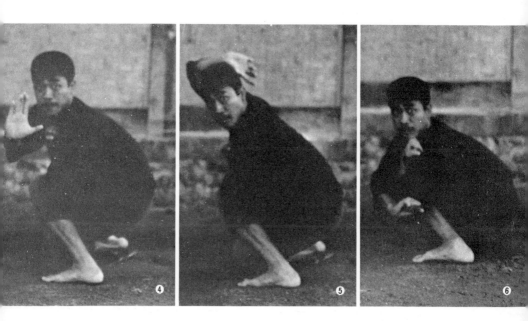

METHOD H. Perisai Diri makes use of the *sempok* position from which to deliver a thrust kicking action. First, assume a *sempok* from the left combative posture (♯1). Then drop your body to the left and front, hugging the ground, supporting yourself with both hands, and letting your left buttock touch the ground; simultaneously deliver a thrust kick with your right leg (♯2). Now spring to your feet as quickly as possible, using the thrust of both arms (action not shown). Since your kick should, obviously, be aimed at some vital portion of the enemy's anatomy (knee, groin, midsection, rib area), the target you choose (if you are dealing with only one enemy) should be to your right and somewhat to the rear. However, if you are confronted by two enemies, you may face directly into one (as in ♯1) and attack the other provided he is behind you and to the right.

METHOD I. Tjingrik exponents of west Java often use the *sempok* in order to rise quickly, aim a false kick, step down, and attack with their arms and hands. From the *sempok* taken from a right combative posture (♯ 1), rise as speedily as possible and fake a kick with your advancing right leg (♯ 2–♯ 3); then step down quickly in a long lunge forward (♯ 4–♯ 5). Of particular importance here are the arm and hand actions based on those of the fighting monkey (*ngrik*) who claws at his enemy's vitals (usually the throat and groin).

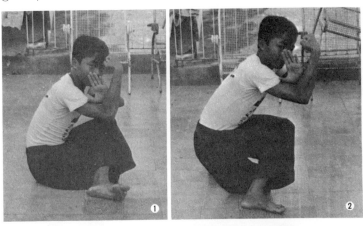

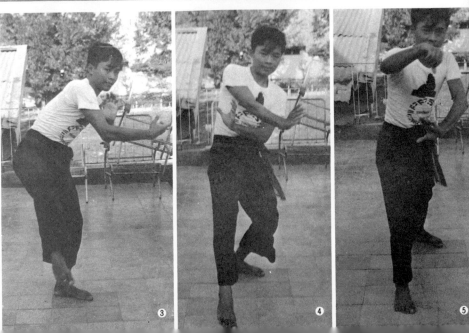

Training Exercise 9

The Perisai Diri exponent makes highly effective use of deceptive hand and arm tactics; following the style's characteristic combative postures, he may have his arms at either a high or low level at the time of the enemy's attack. The following exercises are aimed to develop basic Perisai Diri arm and hand skills for dealing with thrust punches or kicking actions directed toward the groin, midsection, or facial areas. Note that this tactic, although it may be used against either the inside or the outside of the attacking weapon, always prefers the latter since it affords greatest protection.

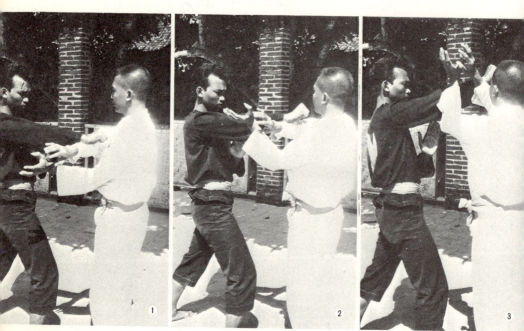

METHOD A. Stand facing your training partner. At his thrust punch (arrowhead fist shown) made with his right arm, and aimed at your midsection, pass both of your arms under his attacking arm, but below his elbow, hands held open (# 1). Swing both of your arms upward together and circularly over against the outside of his attacking right arm; fling his arm off to your right front corner; step in that direction with your right foot to reinforce your arm action (# 2–# 4). Terminate your counteraction by bringing both hands held as tiger claw hands to simulate gouging your partner's eyes or rending his facial areas (# 5–# 6). This sequence is shown from the opposite side to clarify its mechanics (# 7–# 11).

METHOD B. Stand facing your training partner with one arm raised overhead. Let him kick at your midsection using a straight-line forward snap kick, high kick, or heel thrust kick (shown) as in # 1. Just before his attacking foot arrives on target, swing both of your arms against the outside of his kicking leg (right shown) and sweep it forcefully away, by use of your open hands (palms contacting his leg), to your right front corner and downward; step forward with your right foot in the direction you swing your arms (# 2–# 3).

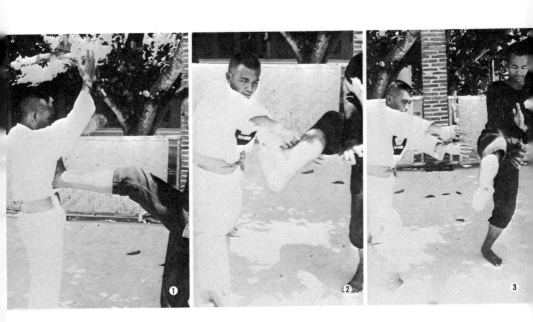

METHOD C. As you face your training partner, he thrusts his right arrowhead fist toward your midsection or facial area, lunging forward to reinforce it. Move your left foot out wide to your left front as you pass your right arm under his attacking arm; raise your free left arm overhead, keeping the elbow slightly bent, hand open (# 1). Parry his attack to your right and downward as you bring your right arm circularly against his arm; twist your hips a bit to your right to reinforce your arm action (# 2–# 3). After completing the parrying action, your right arm provides a covering action so that the enemy cannot attack again with his right arm unless he first disengages it; your left arm remains held high, palm open as a threat to his facial areas (# 4). This sequential action showing a full view of the bodies is illustrated in # 6 and # 7. Study the details of this important evasion tactic from a different camera angle (# 8–# 11). The tactic works well against kicking attacks (# 5).

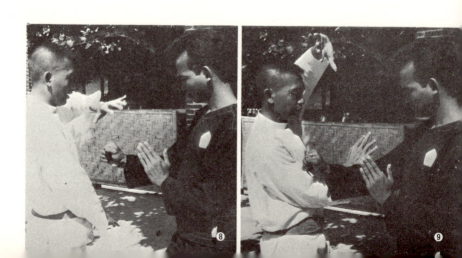

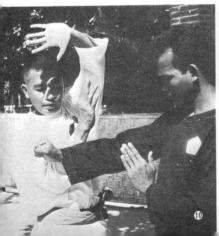

TRAINING EXERCISE 10

This simple Perisai Diri method is used as basic training to develop a coordinated shoulder blocking shock effect and groin attack.

METHOD. Stand quartering into your training partner, using a right combative posture; your right arm hangs downward, protecting your groin as your left arm is held raised, bent at the elbow, hand open, palm facing your partner at the level of your right breast (# 1). Step directly between your partner's legs with your right foot and lunge your body into him so that your shoulder contacts his chest bone or solar plexus (# 2). Drive hard enough to knock him backwards, off-balance (# 3). As he topples, extend your right arm, hand held as a fist; simulate striking him in the groin with a back or bottom fist (# 4); be prepared to deliver successive blows to his groin and even be ready to butt him in the face with your head if he doubles forward.

TRAINING EXERCISE 11

Perisai Diri exponents use this exercise to develop rapid responses to close infighting tactics. A rhythmic exercise, linking those skills learned earlier to yet another action, the entire sequence provides a valuable drill.

METHOD. Face your training partner. As he lunges forward and thrusts his right arrowhead fist at your midsection, execute the evasive action of Training Exercise 9 (page 92–3), as shown in # 1. Your partner continues his attack by trying to drive his shoulder into your midsection and then striking you in the groin with his back or bottom fist (shown) as you back away (he is using Training Exercise 10, page 94) just as is shown in # 2. At his attack, jump lightly to your left rear corner by pivoting on your left foot and carrying your right leg around behind you. Both of your hands push simultaneously, knife edges against his attacking right arm, just above the elbow (# 3). Use his force of attack as resistance to propel yourself backwards into a left combative posture; use both of your hands held open, knife edges facing your partner, anticipating further attack (# 4).

Training Exercise 12

This is a composite exercise which takes the single skills learned in Training Exercises 9–C (page 92) and 11 (page 95), adding to them one more evasive tactic. This exercise is typically one of the Perisai Diri style. It must be done with staccato rhythm.

METHOD: Evade your partner's right arm thrust to your mid-section or face (# 1). As he continues his attack, trying to butt you with his shoulder and strike a fist into your groin, evade him again (# 2–# 3). These are the precise actions of

Training Exercise 11 (page 95). From your partner's position in # 3, he tries to backhand you with his right elbow or fist. As he does this, jump forward around behind his right side, stepping with your right leg first; block his attacking right arm with your left hand, palm open, and/or your right forearm, pushing hard against his attacking arm from above his elbow (# 4). As he turns clockwise to face you, move quickly once again around his right side and to his rear (# 5). As he turns again, both of you come finally face to face; your combative posture is that of the tiger, his that of the dragon (# 6).

TRAINING EXERCISE 13

This is another Perisai Diri exercise designed to develop the evasive skills described at the beginning of Training Exercise 12, but completing that maneuver with more severe measures.

METHOD A. At any appropriate time, as you complete the jumping tactic described in Training Exercise 12 (♯ 4), hook your left hand in beak hand fashion (see ♯ 1 and Fig. 6) around the left side of your partner's neck, at the same time lifting your right leg (♯ 2). Step to your right and swing your partner circularly to your left rear as you put your right foot onto the ground. After he falls, finish him with a knife-edge hand strike to his neck or to the side of his head (♯ 3).

METHOD B. As preparation for the toppling action, put your left hand to his face and with a tiger claw hand simulate a gouging action to the eyes and soft tissues of his face (# 4).

99

METHOD C. Again, using the tiger claw hand, grasp your partner's head with both hands and swing him backward to the ground; simulate twisting his neck with a sharp wrenching action (#1–#3). #4 illustrates the Harimau pentjak-silat equivalent.

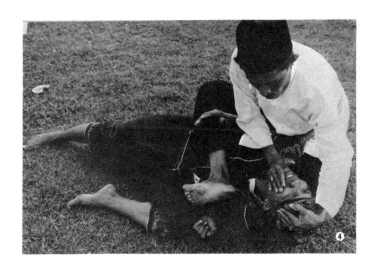

Training Exercise 14

A Perisai Diri countermeasure to the tactic described in Training Exercise 13–A, this exercise continues Training Exercise 12.

METHOD. You and your training partner face each other; he is in a right "dragon" combative posture, his right arm raised high; you are in a "tiger" combative posture, both hands raised defensively in front of you, palms open (# 1).

Your partner leaps around your left side and tries to hook your neck with his right hand preparatory to pulling you to the ground (# 2–# 3). You counter with an evasive wheeling action, turning quickly to your right, pivoting on your right foot, and coming around 180° to escape his pull (# 4–# 5). Protect your body with your hands to avoid a possible kicking attack from him. If he assumes a new combative posture (such as in # 6) and if you rush at him in a straight-line fashion, you may fall victim to a side thrust kick (# 7).

This Mustika Kwitang exercise demonstrates how exponents of that style deliver their particular version of a punching action to the enemy's midsection, and at the same time it shows the trainee how to develop correct breath control and muscular contraction to enable him to withstand the punch. In order to understand this exercise, the trainee must realize that the standard thrust punching action of Mustika Kwitang differs from that of most other styles in that the punching arm is never fully extended (# 1). For that reason, many pentjak-silat countermeasures that are effective against a fully extended punching arm fail when the enemy is a Mustika Kwitang exponent. The punch is delivered by an arm positioned alongside the operator, fist held palm facing the body just below breast level and well forward of the hip. The fist does not smash completely into the target but stops a bit short of a full-arm extension in a particular position that might be called an upright fist, or a standing fist. This method of punching requires that the operator be a bit closer to his target than if he were using a fully extended arm.

METHOD. The receiver of the attack assumes a straddle stance, upright, arms hanging naturally at his sides; he does nothing to counter the punch about to be delivered by his training partner, who places himself so that he needs to take only one step forward (right step illustrated) to strike the target correctly. The target area should be that of the hard stomach muscles, not the solar plexus (# 2–# 3). The power of the punch must, of course, be built up gradually, so that it may finally be delivered and withstood at maximum strength and velocity. The partner who is to receive the attack balances solidly on both legs; he takes a full breath, swelling his abdominal region, then releases a small amount of air and tenses his stomach muscles.

Combat Situations

The sampling of basic pentjak-silat tactics that follows, although presented in the form of hypothetical combat, is based on realistic occurrences that are fairly common. The situations and responses are intended to be utilized for purposes of self-defense, to be sure, but many of the situations may be put, just as they are shown, to the uses of sport (as for *karate-dō*), while others may be modified with the same aim in mind.

Each of the tactics described is typical of the pentjak-silat style from which it has been taken. It is, therefore, by no means the only solution to the given combative situation, since every other style would have its own answer to the problem; the answer given may, in fact, not even be the best—but it will, nonetheless, be found effective, and it is representative of its particular style: its exponents found it adequate to meet the situation described.

Although pentjak-silat is a defensive art, it recognizes the truth of the old adage that "the best defense is a good offense". In some of the situations that follow, therefore, the fighter designated as the defender will be found to be more nearly an aggressor than the enemy he faces. The trainee

106

should have no difficulty distinguishing between the offensive and defensive actions of the designated defender.

The combative action in this final chapter is intended to suggest the "silat" part of pentjak-silat—in other words, the real fight; but in actuality, for reasons of safety, only the high-spirited but controlled pentjak action has been photographed. It is nonetheless distinct from the pentjak-silat training exercises of the preceding chapter in the sense that all the photographs are of free-fighting action. It is based on the training exercises, and is, in fact, an application of the skills that they are designed to impart. It is obvious that without adequate knowledge of the training exercises, and sufficient practice in them, there can be no free-fighting pentjak skills—nor any effective silat. For these reasons, the reader is strongly advised to master the previous chapters thoroughly before he attempts the combative situations and actions described in this final chapter.

Where the combative situation is based on a particular training exercise, reference to that exercise will be given; if there is no reference, the trainee may go ahead with the combative action without directly consulting the preceding chapter—but he must realize that a thorough knowledge of its contents is essential to skillful action in the situations that follow.

SUMATRAN STYLES

Situation 1. Your enemy having taken a right stance and being momentarily motionless, you, the defender (right) have stepped into a deep right stance to quarter away from him, apparently exposing the back of your right side (# 1). *References:* Training Exercises 7 (page 74), 8-H (page 86), and 4 (page 68).

Action: Whirl to your left, using your right leg as a pivot, and attempt a reverse sickle heel kick into your enemy's midsection, head (as illustrated), or groin (# 2). Your enemy evades your kick by swaying backward just out of range; you complete your whirling action through a half circle and then take to the ground, where, using your right hand as a support, you roll your body over and sit down with your

legs extended (♯ 3). Your enemy counterattacks immediately, kicking at your head with his trailing left leg; you evade the kick by the combined action of slightly twisting your body to the left and parrying his leg in toward his centerline with your right hand, held open; your left hand, placed on the ground, supports this evasive tactic, and your left leg, at the same time, is drawn up (♯ 4). Your parrying action having spun the enemy around to his right, he tries to take advantage of the momentum by making a half circle, using his left leg as a pivot, in order to reverse sickle heel kick you in the head with his right leg; before he can complete the turn, drive a hard side thrust kick with your right foot into his groin (♯ 5). If you cannot reach his groin, make your target the inside of his left thigh at the rear, just above the knee. Either contact should topple him.

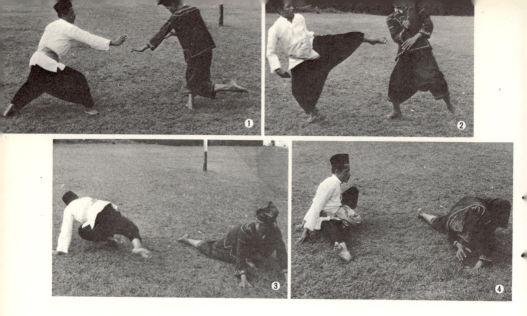

Situation 2. You and your enemy square off in right stances (♯ 1); he sees you moving to the right and attacks by kicking with his trailing left leg.

Reference: Training Exercise 7 (page 74).

Action A: Using his left leg, he aims a roundhouse kick at your right side or midsection which you avoid by stopping your forward movement and pivoting back around to your left (♯ 2). The pursuing enemy quickly puts his left leg to the ground in front of you, where, using it as a pivot, he whirls around backwards to his right in an attempt to aim a right foot reverse sickle heel kick at your back; this you evade by going into a forward lunge step (left knee up), dropping to the ground, using both hands for support in front of you, and keeping an eye on your enemy (♯ 3). When his reverse sickle action misses its target, he follows its momentum into a crouching position, facing you; remain on the ground and continue to watch him but lower body still further (♯ 4). The enemy now attempts to rise (♯ 5–♯ 6). As he does, you leap into him and knock him backward to the ground, completing your response to the situation by clawing his face or some other appropriate action (♯ 7).

110

Action B: This follows the action given above until your enemy begins to rise from the ground (♯ 8), at which point you spring high into the air to hurl your body against him after he is upright. You may, at the same time, find the opportunity to aim a side thrust kick at his midsection, groin, or kneecap (♯ 9).

Situation 3. You and your enemy circle each other in a clockwise manner; he closes in on you, threatening a kicking attack (♯ 1–♯ 2).

References: Training Exercises 4 (page 68), 5 (page 70), 6 (page 72), 7 (page 74), 8–A (page 77), and 8–C (page 79).

Action: Sink to the ground, using your right hand for support and fold your right leg beneath you, your instep behind your left knee (♯ 3). As your enemy approaches for the kick, swing your right leg free from under you and fake a forward movement with it toward him, at the same time continuing to support yourself on your right hand (♯ 4). Now shift your weight onto your left leg, turning your body to the right as you execute a fake reverse sickle heel kick with your right leg to stop the enemy's kick (thrust type shown in the illustration) as well as his advance (♯ 5). As he dodges to his left, lower yourself quickly to the ground onto your right buttock, your weight thrown well forward, and your left leg bent, foot well up under your left buttock (♯ 6); continue to support yourself on your right arm. Swing your left leg in roundhouse fashion, using a hard frontal sickle instep kick, at the enemy's platform right leg; drop your buttocks to the

ground, support yourself on your right elbow and forearm, rolling a bit to your right to do this. Your enemy dodges by quickly shifting his weight and raising the attacked leg (# 7). Putting his right foot to the ground again, the enemy now pivots on it so that he faces you and delivers an immediate thrust kick with his left leg; use your left hand to parry or block the kick if necessary, but your chief evasive action should be change of posture; move away from the kick by stepping your left leg across the front of your body and over your right leg, which rests on the ground; pull yourself into a more upright position and support your body once again on your right hand (# 8). The relentless enemy now jumps in toward you, hopping on his platform right leg, to deliver still another forward thrust kick with his left leg; this you evade by lying back, supporting yourself on your right elbow and parrying the kick upward with your left arm (#.9). The subsequent action—delivering a side thrust kick upward into the enemy's groin with your left leg or a thrust into his right knee from the inside to knock him down—is shown in the sketch.

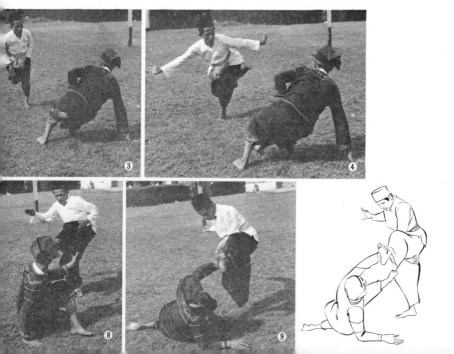

Situation 4. You are in a deep crouch as your enemy advances in an upright posture; when he is near enough, your right hand makes a grab at his advancing left ankle in an attempt to topple him (# 1).

Reference: Training Exercise 4 (page 68).

Action: Against the possible threat of a straight-line frontal snap kick with the enemy's trailing right leg, you rock back and cover yourself with your hands (# 2). The enemy takes advantage of your slight withdrawal and grabs your left

ankle with his right hand as he drops to the ground, and brings your left leg upward, thus toppling you backward (♯ 3). He cleverly blocks your left leg with his left foot and prepares to rise a bit in order to deliver a forward snap kick into your face or midsection. You begin your counterattack by supporting yourself on your left elbow and swinging your right leg in roundhouse fashion (♯ 4). Deliver a hard frontal sickle kick with your right leg at his head (♯ 5) ; a thrust kick may also be used.

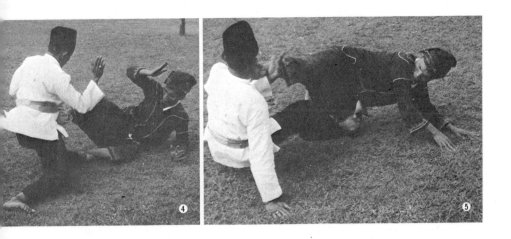

Situation 5. You lie alertly on the ground on your left side, your right leg extended toward your enemy who is approaching with caution (♯ 1).

References: Training Exercises 6 (page 72) and 7 (page 74).

Action: As the enemy draws nearer, withdraw your right leg and change your position so that you are stomach down by turning to your left; move your left foot, leg bent, well forward as you keep watching the enemy (♯ 2–♯ 3). Now roll quickly to the right and, swinging your left leg in short round-house fashion, try to connect a frontal sickle heel kick with your enemy's knees or groin (♯ 4); this action will bring you around onto your left side, facing the enemy, and as you come into that position immediately thrust-drive your left foot at his advancing leg, using his knee as the target. The enemy has evaded your sickle and thrust kicks by disengaging his advanced leg, so draw up your right leg in order to

deliver a forward snap kick, roundhouse kick, or thrust kick if he should approach any nearer; the enemy evades this threat by dropping low to the ground (♯ 5). Sit up and withdraw by bringing your legs up under you, rising into a deep crouch in order to meet the enemy as he rises (♯ 6– ♯ 7). Maintaining the low crouch, turn squarely into him (♯ 8) and fake a deceptive forward step, as though you were about to jump at him. Having anticipated that forward movement, the enemy has responded by delivering a reverse sickle heel kick in the hope of catching you in the groin or midsection as you come forward; he uses his left leg to attack, pivoting on his right; you evade the attack by thrusting your whole body forward under him, feet first, kicking him in the groin as he is midway through his reverse sickle kick action (♯ 9).

Situation 1. You and your enemy are within kicking and grasping range; both of you stand on your right legs, with your raised left legs bent at the knee as though ready to kick. You make a decoy forward snap kick with your left foot, and the enemy, in attempting to evade it, prepares to parry or block it downward with his left arm; as a result you have been able to grasp his left fingers. The enemy draws up his left leg to protect his groin (# 1).

Reference: Training Exercise 3 (page 66).

Action: Retracting your left leg, which has been engaged in the decoy action, bring it back to your left rear corner in a wide forceful sweep-step action and at the same time pull the enemy, with a snap, to his right front corner by using the

combined power of your right hand and body. He should, at this, lose balance and lurch forward, placing his right hand down in front of him to save himself from falling; double his left arm up behind him in hammerlock fashion using your left arm placed over the back of his captured arm to assist the action (♯ 2). His reaction will be to rise, moving forward and pulling against the force you are exerting; as he does, take hold of his captured left arm at the wrist with your left hand, simultaneously kicking against the inside of his extended left leg with your right heel; with a powerful snap you can drag him to the ground where he can be finished with a knife-edge hand against his spine (neck) and/ or his face can be smashed into the ground by the action of your left hand against the back of his head (♯ 3–♯ 4).

Situation 2. Engaged with your enemy at close quarters, you have managed to capture his right arm, as shown (♯ 1).

Action: Take a wide step on your left foot to your left front corner and with both arms snap-pull the enemy to the ground; then immediately release your grip on his arm and take hold of his head in your hands (♯ 2). You may now complete the action in one of two ways. One is to twist his neck sharply around to his left as you hurl him to your own left and to the ground, where further twisting would result in breaking his neck (♯ 3). The other way would be to release his neck (as shown in ♯ 2), and the instant he crumples onto his right side, drop quickly to the ground onto your own right side, away from him, but close enough to deliver a hard thrust kick into his head with your left leg (♯ 4).

Situation 3. You and your enemy have faced each other in right stances; he closes in on you, swinging his trailing left leg in a low straight-legged kick at your groin or kneecap.
Reference: Training Exercise 5 (page 70).
Action A: At his kick, retreat by withdrawing your advanced right leg, keeping your weight well forward and assuming a left lunge stance; simultaneously swing both arms in front of you, starting wide from your left; hold both hands open, with your palms to the left, so that your knuckles face inward toward the coming target—that is, your enemy's left leg, now attacking (#1). Swing your left hand hard, forming an inverted reverse fist on impact with the enemy's inner shinbone; the action should be that of a whiplash. Keep your right hand prepared to reinforce blocking action, or continue other countermeasures.
Action B: After successfully blocking, as described in Action A, go immediately into a counterattack. Deliver a frontal leg sickle attack with your withdrawn right leg, swinging it in roundhouse fashion. You do not aim at the enemy's advanced left leg until after he has stepped down and has put weight on it. Then use your instep to hook around the outside and behind, just above the ankle or the back of his knee, to reap him off of his feet by a strong hooking action to your left (# 2). Note that the enemy has succeeded in disengaging his left leg (the leg which you were attacking) and has brought it back. Your sickle action, thus, was a bit too late, but it did serve to prevent the enemy from further attacks, such as kicking you with his right leg. Note also that he made use of a reinforced open hand tactic to block your sickle leg.

Situation 1. The enemy, having struck at your midsection or face with a right-arm lunge punch, does not immediately withdraw the attacking arm (# 1).

Action A: Dodge the attack by moving outside the enemy's right arm, and step forward and to your left on your right foot, catching his attacking arm near the wrist with your right hand (use a from-the-top grasp, thumb down). Hold your left hand open near your chest, ready to block any kick action he may initiate. Continue your movement around the outside of the enemy's right arm by pivoting on your right foot and placing your left well behind his advanced right foot; you and your enemy now face in approximately the same direction. With your right hand pull his attacking arm in toward you and at the same time drive your left fist, forearm, or elbow into his right elbow just above the joint; then quickly slip your left arm under his captured right arm (# 2) and go on with your counteraction in any of the following ways:

    a. Lift your enemy's right arm and lower your hips as you deliver a hard left elbow side strike to his rib cage or midsection (# 3).

    b. Disengage your right hand grip, keeping that arm

122

in readiness to block his right arm should it be used against you, and push him away from you with your left hand placed just above his right elbow or drive a left spear hand into his throat or eyes (# 4).

c. Move further behind him and bring his captured right arm down, keeping your right grasp as you pull his arm in toward your body. Place your left leg deeply between his legs from the rear and wedge your left hip tightly against the right half of his lower back. Reach your left hand up and around his back so as to be free to slap the left side of his head with your left palm or to strike the outside of his left shoulder (# 5–# 6). He will respond by raising his left arm, and as he does, jerk him forward with your right hand and put your left arm under his left armpit so that you can run that arm up behind his neck. You may now force him to the ground by bearing downward against his upper body with your left arm and moving your right leg in front of him all the while retaining your right-hand grasp of his right arm; if you now lock both his arms, your left hand is in a position to push down against the back of his trapped right arm (# 7–# 8).

3

4

5

6

7

Action B: As the enemy makes his right lunge punch, step back on your right leg and drop quickly onto your right knee, out of range of the punch. Keep your opened left hand in front of you to protect your face; your right hand, resting lightly on the ground, is not intended to support you (# 1). This position is, in fact, a ruse, the purpose of which is to induce the enemy to close with you by attacking with a forward snap kick, using his trailing left leg. When he does so, you must be quick to respond. Rise as the kick comes toward you, jumping forward onto your left foot and thrusting your left hand, held in the form of a crane fist, downward and hard into his groin (# 2–# 4). If your groin attack has

stopped him or toppled him backward, step forward on your right leg and deliver a straight snap kick into his groin with your right foot (action not illustrated). If your groin attack has not been altogether successful, you must be prepared to block the continued forward motion of his left leg kicking action by driving both elbows into his upraised left knee, just above the kneecap (♯ 5). It is also possible that even if your groin attack is successful (♯ 4), he will shift his weight back onto his left leg and attempt a kicking or kneeing action with his right leg; should he do so, scoop the leg up into your arms and heave him backwards (♯ 6).

JAVANESE STYLES

Situation 1. Your enemy has aimed his left fist, in a thrust punch, at your face.

Action: You dodge his attack by stepping forward circularly to your right, around his attacking arm, to face him at about a 45° angle, placing both hands, held as knife edges, against the outside of his thrusting arm so as to block it above the elbow (#1). Step forward on your left leg placing your foot in front of him; at the same time, using both arms, press his attacking arm in toward his centerline and a bit downward. Now disengage your right hand, meanwhile continuing your blocking action with your left hand, which acts as a cover (#2). With your free arm deliver a knife hand blow to the back of his head or the nape of his neck (#3).

Situation 2. You are in a right stance, your enemy in a left; you face each other; he attacks by punching and kicking consecutively with his right arm and leg.

Action A : Since the punch precedes the kick, you must parry that first, using the palm of your right hand to turn his arm in toward his centerline; keeping your groin covered with your left hand, move your right foot a bit to the right (# 1). As his roundhouse kick arrives, step inside of it on your left leg; disengage your right hand from his arm and scoop up the attacking right leg from the inside, just above the ankle; you must hold your palm upward as you lift his leg upward; step forward onto your left leg to reinforce your lifting action (# 2). Now using your left leg as a platform, move forward and deliver a hard straight snap kick with your trailing right leg directly into his groin.

Action B: If your right-handed parrying action against his attacking right arm prevents the enemy from continuing a kicking attack, reinforce your parry by stepping forward on your left foot in the direction of the parry, grasp his right wrist firmly, and pull him forward (♯ 2). His reaction will be to try to straighten up and to pull back, away from your right hand grip. This you permit him to do, at the same time putting your left foot behind his right leg (♯ 3) and accelerating his backward movement by the combined force of your left arm thrusting against his upper body or face; release your right-hand grip as you do this (♯ 4).

128

Situation 1. Your enemy is simultaneously aiming a right lunge punch at your midsection and is advancing his right leg around and behind your own right leg (# 1).

Reference: Training Exercise 15 (page 104).

Action: As the enemy lunges forward, shift your weight onto your left leg, raising your left arm high and keeping your right arm low (# 2). Before he has time to land his punch, you must kick your free right leg back and out against the side of his advancing right leg; at the same time, chop your left arm downward, knife edge against the inner side of his attacking forearm, while your right hand, also knife-edged, swings to deliver a blow to his neck or head (# 3). Shift to the left and wheel him to the ground, finishing him with a hard knife edge of one or both hands to his solar plexus (# 4–# 5).

Situation 2. The enemy is lunging forward with a right knife-edge blow (not shown) to your head or neck; you meet his attack from a left stance (figure on the left) (# 1).

Action: Before the enemy has time to land his knife-edge attack, counterattack from your left stance with a right-hand punch to his midsection, covering the left side of your head with your left hand, held open (# 2). This latter action successfully blocks the enemy's knife-edge attack to the left side of your head, while he, for his part, also successfully blocks your punch to his midsection with his left hand held open (# 3). Break the stalemate by flinging both arms upward and high overhead, an action designed to throw both of his arms outward; shift your weight to your left leg, and using it as a platform, deliver a hard forward snap kick to the enemy's groin (# 4–# 5)

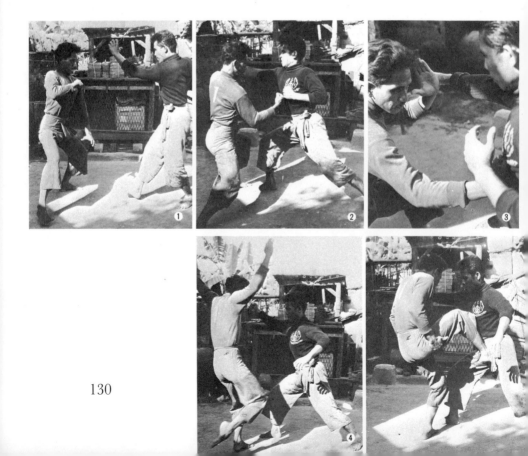

Situation 1. As your enemy moves forward to deliver a kicking action with his right leg, you face him with a cross-legged stance, your weight equally balanced on your legs, as though you had just risen from a posture of sitting on the ground. Your left leg is in front of your right, and the toes of your left foot are turned outward, forming a right angle to your right foot (♯ 1).

Reference: Training Exercise 8–B (page 78).

Action A: If the enemy is using either a straight snap kick or a roundhouse type of kicking attack, aimed at the groin or higher, you must immediately shift your weight to your right foot, bring your left leg around and behind, and simultaneously turn your body to the left, stretching your right arm out so as to catch the enemy's attacking right leg from underneath, palm upward and near the calf (♯ 2). Now pull the enemy's leg in the direction of the kick and bring your left leg deep behind your right, near the outside of the enemy's right foot, with your toes pointing in the same direction as his (♯ 3). Shift your weight onto your newly positioned left and drive your right foot (or knee) hard into the enemy's groin (♯ 4).

Action B: If the enemy's kick is near the side-thrust type, shift your weight onto your left leg and quickly raise your right leg (possible target) to protect your groin; you then strike your upper wrist bone hard against the enemy's kicking foot, just above the ankle (# 2–# 3). You may then knock the enemy's attacking leg inward, toward his center-line, and deliver a thrust kick of your own to the kneecap of the enemy's platform leg; or else you may face into the enemy at once and deliver a straight snap kick into the groin.

Situation 2. You have assumed a posture of sitting on the ground while the enemy is on his feet and is closing in on you (♯ 1).

Reference: Training Exercise 4 (page 68).

Action: When the enemy comes within range, meet his attack with a roundhouse kick aimed at his head, using your right leg (♯ 2). Should he evade the kick (♯ 3), leap to your feet in order to face him from some suitable combative posture (not shown).

Situation 3. You are in a right stance, and your enemy aims a right lunge punch at your face.

Action A: Quickly duck under the enemy's right arm and step forward on your left foot. Deliver either a short right thrust punch to his ribs or solar plexus (# 1) or a right forward elbow strike to these same areas (# 2). Immediately after impact, hook your right foot inside the enemy's right foot and scoop his right leg in toward you (# 3–# 4); now grab the enemy's right leg with both hands and lift it up and to the right powerfully enough to send him sprawling face down to the ground (# 5).

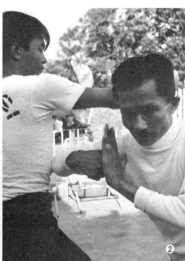

Action B: At the enemy's right thrust punch, take a wide step to your left, bringing your left foot a bit forward; at the same time, parry the attacking arm from the outside with your opened left hand, palm placed against his arm just below the elbow, to your right (# 1). Parry the arm downward, striking hard with your right hand, knife-edged, into his facial area or neck (# 2–# 3). Alternatively, you may use your hand as shown in # 4 and # 5.

Situation 4. Your enemy is moving to his left in preparation for some new attack. Deliberately swing your right leg in a slow, high kick aimed at his midsection. *He must see the kick coming*, and he must not suppose it to be so weak that he can ignore it; accordingly, he dodges to his left (♯ 1–♯ 2).

Action: Put the foot with which you feinted the kicking attack quickly to the ground, placing it behind the enemy's trailing left foot (♯ 3). Keeping your right arm in readiness to block any action he may take, scoop up his trailing left leg with both your hands and at the same time drive your right shoulder into his buttocks (♯ 4). The combination of catching his leg and your forward body motion will knock him sprawling onto his face (♯ 5).

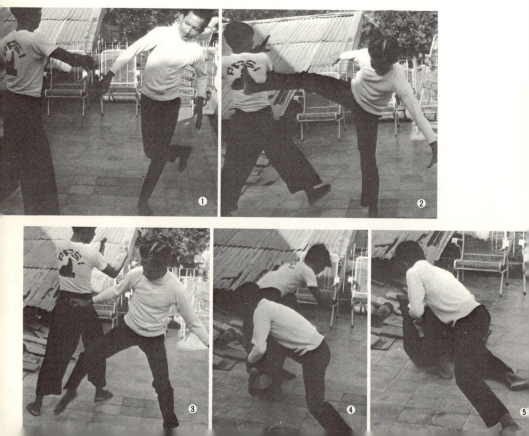

Situation 5. You have assumed a left stance, with the toes of your left foot pointing left; although your weight is equally centered, your right flank is exposed; your enemy is going to attack (# 1).

Action: Pivot as though you were turning to walk away from his oncoming attack, moving your right leg across and ahead of your left (# 2). To lure the enemy onward, you continue your retreat by stepping forward, putting your left foot ahead of your right and twisting your body to the left to watch the enemy (# 3). You not only let him narrow the gap between you, you narrow it yourself by faking another forward step with your right foot, bringing it in line with your platform left foot; after delaying a bit, to be sure that the enemy has closed, drive a hard thrust kick backward with your right leg into his groin or advancing knee, twisting your body to the right as you kick (# 4).

Situation 1. You and your enemy have squared off, both in right stances, and you have managed to get your right foot behind his as preparation for an old tactic well known to most combatants (# 1).

Reference: Training Exercise 7 (page 74).

Action: By driving forward with all your weight, you hope to press down your enemy's trapped right leg (# 2). At the same time, you lunge and twist your body a bit to the left; the combination may succeed in making him lose his balance (# 3). But whether he falls or not, you complete the attack by delivering a reverse sickle heel kick, aiming at his head if he has fallen (not shown) or at his groin if he has managed to regain his balance (# 4).

Situation 2. You enemy has delivered a strong right side thrust kick at your midsection (♯ 1).

Action A: Dodge the focus of his kick by stepping back to your left rear corner onto your left foot; position yourself on the outside of his leg, twisting your body slightly to meet the attack. Simultaneously slide your right arm, the hand held open, under the attacking leg, just below the knee, making hard impact contact with the inner edge of your forearm and lifting the leg upward so as to keep the enemy pinned on his platform left leg and unable to withdraw his attacking leg (♯ 2). Take a deep step toward the enemy, raising his right leg even higher with your right arm as you meanwhile slide your left arm over the uppermost part of his right thigh, pressing downward at the hip; place your left leg across and in front of the enemy's platform leg so as to block any movement he might try to make with it (♯ 3). Heave him to the ground by the combined power of your upward lift and downward press and wheeling action; he will revolve around and over your extended left leg (not shown).

Action B: Evade the focus of the enemy's kick by taking a wide step directly to the left, bringing your body well outside the range of the attack. Swing a rising roundhouse kick into the enemy's groin from underneath his attacking right leg (# 2).

Action C: Another method is to evade the focus of the kick by taking a step to the left, around the outside of the enemy's attacking leg but a bit in toward him, while at the same time pushing the back of his attacking leg, below the knee, with the palm of your left hand (# 3). Then take a quick, short step closer in, on your left foot, placing it behind his platform foot and deliver a palm heel strike directly into his groin (# 4).

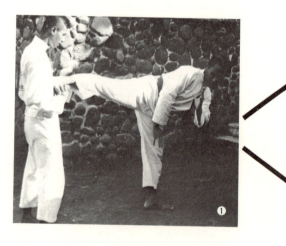

BALINESE STYLE

BHAKTI NEGARA PENTJAK-SILAT

Situation. Your enemy has contrived to get a firm grip on your right arm and has twisted it counterclockwise (from your point of view), rotating your arm with the thumb downward as if to obtain an armlock on you; you are in a right stance (# 1–# 2).

Action: Slide your opened left hand down your own right arm and onto your enemy's right wrist, pushing hard against his grip (# 2–# 3). Making use of the combined strength of both arms, pull hard to draw the enemy in toward you, and at the same time raise the elbow of your

captured right arm; pull your left hand hard back in toward you and down to cause the enemy's grip to slip from your wrist onto your hand (# 4). As the enemy loses his grip of your wrist, pass your right arm, elbow first, over the top of his right arm at the bend of the elbow, at the same time lowering your hips; should the enemy attempt to use his left hand to reinforce his failing right-hand grasp on your right hand, do not try to prevent him (# 4–# 5); your left hand grips the enemy's right wrist. Once your right arm is free, slide it under his armpit and onto his captured right arm, above the elbow (# 6). Dig the fingers of your right hand into his throat; the entwined arm acts as a kind of lock, and you could easily, at this point, throttle the enemy (# 7).

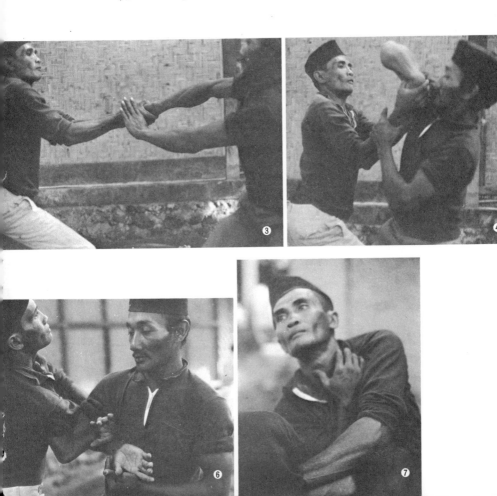

HARIMAU

PATAI

SETIA HATI

SUMATRA

BARU

Djakarta

JAVA

KUMANGO

PERISAI DIRI

TJINGRIK